Getting Business Fit

By Gary King

find ◦ improve ◦ track

iUniverse, Inc.
New York   Bloomington

iUniverse books may be ordered through booksellers or by contacting:

iUniverse
1663 Liberty Drive
Bloomington, IN 47403
www.iuniverse.com
1-800-Authors (1-800-288-4677)

ISBN: 978-1-4401-3668-9 (sc)
ISBN: 978-1-4401-3669-6 (ebook)

Printed in the United States of America

iUniverse rev. date: 05/19/2009

Praise for Gary King

"When my company and one we acquired merged, we did not have a formal quality program and lacked a standardized approach to continuous improvement. Gary took the reins and led a cross-functional team to design and roll-out an enterprise-wide process that enabled all team members, regardless of their role in the organization, to contribute and participate in identifying and implementing sustainable business process improvements. Employees, clients and the company were all winners as client satisfaction increased, costs went down and employees were rewarded for their efforts. What Gary created was not just a program, but a way to help people think differently about how they do their jobs. He truly made a difference." *Valerie Bonebrake, Executive Vice President, Chief Logistics Officer*

"Gary is one of the best people I have worked with during my professional career. He is always focused, providing a clear direction and sense of purpose to his teams. Gary also makes a point of always recognizing good work and not taking people for granted, which is a special skill for someone at his level." *Kathleen (Canning) Bubniak, Manager, North America Quality Systems and Process Integration*

"I was privileged to work with Gary when he spearheaded our successful ISO Certification initiative, which was achieved in a very short time frame even though we started from scratch. I also worked with Gary when he led a very successful continuous improvement initiative for a very large and demanding customer. This same program was then rolled out across the entire company. I have always found Gary to be very knowledgeable and could depend on Gary to offer wise counsel on all business issues." *Steve Wilson, Director, Supply Chain Engineering; Director, Operations*

"Gary was very instrumental in helping me start up a warehouse operation for Samsung's largest Distribution Center. As the Manager of this operation I looked to Gary for support and ideas for continuous improvement. Gary was always willing to help and get personally involved or point me in the right direction. He is a great resource with a lot of industry knowledge. Very energetic and upbeat, always smiling. He helped me take on my challenges as if they were his own." *Ray Schiliro, Distribution Center Manager*

"In my time working with Gary I was impressed by his straightforward approach to projects that brought value to our customers. Gary has several qualities that are important: attention to detail, the ability to communicate clearly and consistently, strong analytical thinking, and consultative approach focused on driving quality initiatives. I can personally attest to the fact that through Gary's consistent and proven approach, he not only uncovered hidden value for our clients, but for the overall organization as well." *John Norris, Senior. Director Business Development*

"I had the pleasure of working with Gary while going through an ISO Certification process. Gary and his team managed this project efficiently and successfully by providing clear instructions to all departments in the organization to achieve our certification. Through Gary's leadership, we understood the benefits of this quality system and were able to accomplish it in manageable steps. Gary is a very positive, ethical and hard working executive who quickly builds rapport and trusting relationships. I hope I have the opportunity to work with him again in my career." *Jill Brinkmann, Director, Human Resources*

"I had the distinct pleasure of working with Gary and found him to be an excellent results-oriented leader that drives for continuous improvement in all aspects of business. Gary is able to create a working environment and strong relationship with his teams that identifies opportunities for improvement and successful efficient solutions. One of the attributes that I admire most about Gary is the support given to his teams in providing the tools and resources necessary to complete their jobs without complicating them with unnecessary or non-value added tasks. Besides being an outstanding senior leader, Gary is an outstanding person with high moral standards and long standing relationships with many colleagues that hold him in the highest regard." *Adam Croskey, Senior Manager Risk and Safety Management*

Dedication

"Great lives are the culmination of great thoughts followed by great actions." —Peter Sinclair

I dedicate this book to my Mom and Dad (Ann and Glenn) who continually filled my mind with great thoughts in order that I might pursue great actions in life. You vowed to love each other through sickness and in health and kept to your promise for 54 years. Being the true soul mates that you are—you both surrendered to Cancer just 13 days apart. I find some comfort in knowing that the two of you are together for eternity but miss you both so much.

Forever your Son...Gary

Acknowledgments

"There are some people, who live in a dream world, and there are some who face reality; and then there are those who turn one into the other." —Douglas Everett

This book would not have been possible without the many challenges, opportunities and individuals that I have come to experience and know throughout my career. Many of the successes that I've endured were truly inspired by individuals with a higher degree of talent and passion for quality and continuous improvement than I could ever strive to achieve in my lifetime. To them I give great thanks and my never ending gratitude for their wisdom and dedication to serve. I believe that our choices in life are greatly inspired by individual and group encounters we experience throughout our lifetime. Each contact produces a spark of light or pinch of darkness within us that shapes our personalities, feelings, likes and dislikes and determines what paths we will choose throughout our life journey. On my journey thus far, I have encountered several who have contributed many sparks of light. Those sparks have consumed the pinches of darkness—coming together to produce a burning passion within me to continually serve and pursue opportunities, to improve my work and the work of others.

Although they are many, there are a few whose spark was just a bit brighter and as a result, they had a profound impact on my choices and inspirations in life. Those few who helped turn my dreams into reality. They include: my Wife Karen who is always there to remind me that I can accomplish anything that I set out to do. You have been extremely supportive and have given me the confidence and courage to accomplish much in life and you instill in me the desire to accomplish so much more. I love you!

John Burns it's been many, many years when I first approached you as a 15 year old on my bike—looking for my first real job. You gave me that opportunity—hiring me on the spot as a Busboy in your Ronardo's Restaurant in San Bernardino, California in April 1973. My starting pay: $1.65 per hour. With tips, I was rich! I was able to buy my first car just months later…an old VW that got me to and from work and school and the drive-in movies. You provided me with memories I will always cherish and a great first job! I miss the seven course meals and working with Tim, Denny, Wayne and Nancy. Oh, and Benji and Chava too!

Don Pugh you were in fact the best boss I ever had. You oversaw a Home Repair program that served senior citizens and low income families within San Bernardino County. I was your Storekeeper but you saw more in me than the confines of issuing and ordering parts and supplies for the repair crews. You said I had great potential and you took it upon yourself to help me discover what that potential might be. You exposed me to many "leadership" opportunities that served as the beginning to my career in executive leadership. Thank you Don!

Emil Marzullo, who was the first boss I ever had that was also a really good friend. Folks say you can't have both (boss and friendship) but you proved them wrong. Through your leadership and friendship we accomplished great things for the County of San Bernardino, Office of Special Districts. You also pushed me to go back to school, which I did and I earned my degree in Business that opened many doors for me down the road that led me to where I am today. Oh and, thanks for hiring me a wife and…my stool still won't go down :-)

My first Mentor *Harry Clark* an extremely brilliant man who saw potential within me that I never knew existed and helped bring it to the surface. I owe my venture into professionalism and a great deal of my career success to you. Thanks Harry!

John Bernard (JB), a great man with strong faith who gave me my first formal start in Quality and Continuous Improvement. John, remember QACT—quality assurance, compliance and training? That was our first real Quality Department that you named! Thanks John—and FYI—there's no Muck in my bag :-)

Bob Whitely, who also believed in my abilities and welcomed me into his operations to put my approach and techniques to the test and helped with their success. You were like a big brother to me—always watching my back. And, you were always there to provoke a good laugh at a time when a good laugh was much needed. I still prefer the side of the bed closest to the door :-)

My good friend and a great President and CEO *Frank Reuwer*—you are greatly missed by so many…a man taken at his prime. You excelled to the level of President and CEO in multiple organizations but never lost sight of the lowest of positions, always taking time to acknowledge individuals at all levels. I miss you Frank… but I'm sure you're kept busy up there in an executive role working for the big guy!

Tom Lilly, another great President and CEO who also saw something in me at a time when I really needed to prove myself to secure my position with an organization challenged with integration and downsizing. You gave me the opportunity to demonstrate my tenacity and perseverance and stood by me while we successfully sought and achieved company-wide ISO 9001: 2000 certification in record time—earning international recognition. Thanks Tom!

Michael Harthcock, who found a way to put compassion for others before business and still succeed in a leadership role. You've made many sacrifices for our country earning two Bronze Stars and if there is a special award for being an all around great guy and true friend, you've earned it many times over. Thanks Michael!

Harold "H" Bender, who was by far the best direct report I've ever had the pleasure to work with. A gentleman with a kind soul and brilliant mind who learned one of life's greatest success secrets—that before you can be a great leader you must first learn to be a great servant. You've easily mastered both and I see great and continued success in your future. Say hello to Susan for me!

Eric Ludewig, who graduated from Syracuse in the morning, threw all your worldly possessions in your truck and drove straight through that same evening to Chicago to begin working with me in your first "quality role" as our Internal ISO Auditor. You have since excelled to where you are today in Quality Management for one of the greatest healthcare product manufacturers in the world. Way to go Eric! I'm still waiting to do lunch…

Ian Farquharson, a business associate who I first met during a formal ISO implementation of whom I've befriended over the years. You have had such a strong impact on me that I can honestly say that this book would not exist had our paths never crossed. A great portion of what I know today about getting business fit I learned through you. If it weren't for the distance between us—you in the UK and me here in Chicago, I believe we would be spending a lot of time (and money) on green fees and swapping stories. Thanks Ian you're a tremendous asset to the ISO process and many organizations have you to thank for their continual business successes.

Denis Reilly, an outstanding President who stuck by me and supported my efforts even at times when we didn't quite see eye-to-eye. You were that strong leadership figure that I needed when I was stubborn—to coach me back down to reality. I learned patients, perseverance and timing from you and for that I thank you!

Jim Ritchie, who became my new boss, President and CEO after the company I worked for was acquired. It was a turbulent time and everyone's jobs from the acquired company (including mine) were on the line. You believed in me and stepped up to support my quality initiatives without hesitation. You "got it" when others just couldn't see the forest through the trees. Your support lead to millions in improvement savings that I received credit for earning a special recognition and a trip to Cancun for me and my wife Karen to enjoy. It was a highlight in my career that I will always cherish. Thank you Jim!

Mike Nattz my first formal executive Mentor. We worked together for several years but our paths only crossed briefly. You agreed to serve as my Mentor while working at Yellow Roadway Corporation, Logistics. In that short time you provided invaluable advice and insight regarding my career. Your wisdom carried me through some challenging times and I thank you for having the great character that you have and being the true professional that you are. Thanks Mike!

Contents

Introduction

"There are two primary choices in life; to accept conditions as they exist, or accept the responsibility for changing them.
—Denis Waitely

Businesses of today—both large and small, have been negatively impacted by global competitiveness and a strained economy. Yesterday's financial challenges that appeared as small blips on the P&L radar are now forcing business leaders to take a harder look at their efficiency and effectiveness. Many have become entrenched in a survival mode scrambling to implement quick cost-cutting measures that have led to drastic cuts in key positions. Vacancies have been left unfilled, succession plans put on hold, discretionary spending capped, customers requiring a greater degree of time and resources to service—abandoned, and worse—businesses that had been around for many decades, closing their doors altogether.

According to many economists our economic conditions are the worst in 30+ years with over 5 million jobs lost since our recession began in late 2007. National unemployment has reached an all time high at over 8% and is anticipated to get as high as 10% by the end of 2009. In addition, those working part-time jobs because they couldn't find full-time work or their hours had been cut back due to slack conditions, jumped to 8 million, the highest since July 1983. And finally, the number of Americans continuing to collect unemployment benefits surged to over 6 million the highest level since 1983.

Another sign of the times is the impact the economy has had on the retail industry. In 2008, numerous retail icons filed for bankruptcy protection and or closed several store locations. When you factor in the backbone of their business, the supply chain, you can imagine the tremendous impact this is having on marketing, sales, manufacturing, transportation, distribution, third party providers and the workforce these service providers employ. Not to mention the billions of dollars in aid being sought after by major financial institutions and the three major auto makers. Few have escaped the woes of our current economy.

On the brighter side we have Obama who may just be that breath of fresh air we desperately need in American politics to bring us out of the doom and gloom and into brighter days. Time will tell…but in the mean time, let's see what we can do as industry leaders to become lean mean competitive machines. Let's step up and take action to help limit the risks that we may be facing in the days, weeks, months and possibly years to come. Know that it will require quick action on your part to wake up and acknowledge that drastic change in your business culture is necessary. Notice I said "quick action" not "quick fixes." Too many American businesses have grown spoiled and given way to complacency which usually results in quick fixes when times get tough. If we continue down this path we'll soon find ourselves walking down the road talking to ourselves and asking what went wrong…?

The Chairman of the Federal Reserve Dr. Ben S. Bernanke recently stated that we will climb out of our recession by the end of 2009 "if" the stimulus plan works and banks start lending again. Top economists are predicting that things are actually going to get worse as this year comes to a close and worsen through 2010 before we see any sign of economic recovery. Are you prepared to gamble on whose right? Are you prepared to endure a continual decline in profits over the next 12 to 18 months? If you are super…but most likely you're not. At best you might be somewhat prepared…but to what degree and for how long? Purchasing this book will not guarantee that your profits will not decline. However, embracing the business fit process will guarantee you bottom-line savings you can take to the bank—if you still have a bank you can rely on.

I've created this book for the executive leader in any organization of any size. I speak to you as I would if we were to sit down and meet face-to-face. I know how precious and limited your time is, so I forego much of the typical rhetoric one might find in any book written for the serious leader. The cut to-the-chase approach is simple, to-the-point and easy to follow so that you can champion measurable results immediately. However, I suggest you don't…instead, I highly recommend that you read this book straight through once, and then read it again, before you choose to take any action. I know, first I acknowledge how precious and limited your time is, and I'm already asking you to set aside your valuable time to read this book not once but twice before you take action. I assure you, this book is an easy read and well worth reading twice. In fact, I would further recommend that you secure copies for members of your leadership team and instruct them to do the same—before you even schedule your first meeting with them to begin step one in getting business fit.

By following the business fit process you will be better equipped to survive the economic woes of today while strengthening your competitive advantage. You will soon abandon your quick fix short-term approach for long-term sustainable growth as you begin your journey in getting business fit.

Getting Business Fit

"More powerful than the will to win is the courage to begin."
—Unknown Author

First things first…we need to educate you…yes… you. By continually delegating the learning experience on to others in your organization because you're too busy or you feel the required commitment of your time is "beneath you" is only distancing yourself from reality. The reality being that <u>you</u> must embrace change and become the example for others in your organization to follow. The degree of success that your business achieves following the business fit process will be measured by the degree to which you embrace the process and adhere to it day in and day out.

The "fit" in getting business fit is an acronym for find the waste, improve the process and track the results. I liken business fitness to our own pursuit of physical and mental fitness. To succeed and prosper in business we must maintain a lean and healthy organization just as we would maintain a lean and healthy body to remain in top physical and mental condition.

Physical Fitness is being able to perform physical activity and having the energy and strength to feel as good as possible. Being fit also lowers our risk for things like heart attacks, diabetes, high blood pressure and some cancers. It can help us sleep better, handle stress better, and keep our minds sharp. Making small changes in our daily lifestyle can improve our physical and mental fitness. When we stay active and fit, we burn more calories. Being fit also enables us to do more physical activity and help manage our weight.

Now, let's take the above paragraph and put a spin on it replacing the reference to our *physical fitness* with *business fitness* to bring you to where I'm at with getting business fit.

Business Fitness is being able to perform work tasks and having the resources and expertise to perform the tasks with the greatest efficiency. Being business fit reduces costs, eliminates waste, enhances customer loyalty and promotes growth. It sustains continual improvement, empowers the workforce and enhances individual development. By continually seeking opportunities to improve processes and develop our workforce we improve the fitness of our business. When we stay focused and fit, we prosper. Being business fit also enables us to do more value added activity and remain customer focused. That's what getting business fit is all about—having the resources and expertise, empowering them to find improvement opportunities, initiating positive change in the status quo, and tracking your measured results to validate success. Getting business fit is also about eliminating complexities, errors, problems and waste within your work processes by pursuing opportunities that lead to simplicity, consistency, value, standardization and best practices. What lies between your current state and best practice is your bridge to fitness the fit process will help you construct. Underneath this great bridge flows a steady stream of endless improvement opportunities. Some of these opportunities represent the low hanging fruit while others represent fruit on the ground. And, yes, these endless improvement opportunities also represent the top-of-the-tree fruit…those that make the climb and reach well worth the extra effort.

My Story

"Think left and think right and think low and think high. Oh, the thinks you can think up if only you try!"—Dr. Seuss

Before we embark on the fit process, I would like to share a personal story that lead to me writing this book. I believe this story also provides a testimony to the success of team work and perseverance at a time when any hope for success had been abandoned. As you read this story, listen for the learning that exist within—such as opportunity, diplomacy, perseverance, teamwork, training, empowerment, communications, documentation, engagement, continuous improvement, best practices, customer satisfaction, customer loyalty, and success. See if you can find where these learnings exist within the story.

Earlier in my career when I was still discovering my passion for quality and continuous improvement I was presented a tremendous challenge. I was hired by a third party logistics (3PL) provider to manage a warehouse operation that serviced a major CPG client. As a result of external audits by our client, forty plus nonconformities or "formal quality incidents" were documented. Our account with them was placed on probation and moving quickly towards termination. The client was already shopping for a new third party provider to transition the account over to. Faced with the extensive list of nonconformities the 3PL that hired me had pretty much given up on the account. I became the good faith effort to try and salvage the account leaning more towards helping to shut the operation down. To add to the challenge on my first day, I was told that my staff was heavily shrouded in a Union environment that leadership believed to be a primary culprit in the downturn of this particular operation. I was also informed that the person I was replacing and who was tasked to "show me the ropes" had already transferred out of the operation. I was on my own. To top it off, my new go to guy, the Operations Supervisor, was out sick for the remainder of the week.

Things were looking pretty gloomy. I was already wondering how I was going to explain to my wife why I quit after only one day on the job. She became that spark of light that I needed when she assured me that everything was going to work out just fine. I recall standing in the Operations Office, where the day's work orders or "pick-sheets" were printed and assigned—waiting for my people to show up. This is where I was told they all gathered at the start of the shift and the best place to meet with them. The first to arrive was the Operations Coordinator. We exchanged brief introductions before he provided me with a quick rundown on how work orders were printed out and assigned. It didn't sound too complicated so I decided to stick around and participate in the process first hand. One by one the workers showed up and the introductions continued as we assigned the various work orders out. This helped ease the obvious tension between me and them—me as I hadn't a clue as to what I was getting myself into and them with the fear of the unknown—was I going to be the boss from hell or a complete push over…or fall somewhere in between.

Meeting them one-on-one and in small groups really helped break the ice. By the time the whole team was gathered, I felt pretty good—they didn't seem as bad or as difficult as I was led to believe they were.

Moving forward, I took an observatory approach to get a feel for how things went. I asked allot of questions of the Operations Coordinator who soon became my right hand person. Little by little throughout the week I approached the workforce to observe their assigned tasks trying not to be overbearing or coming across as micro-managing. I was determined to put forth a sincere effort to know and understand what they did day in and day out and why. When Friday rolled around I decided to make my move—to lay it all out on the line...to be completely up front and honest with my new team as to where we all stood with the account and quite frankly, with our jobs. I needed to hear from them, after all, they were the experts—surely they would know where the real problems and opportunities lied. I asked the team to meet with me right after first break. Instead of taking their breaks as they usually did hanging out in the break room, they all crowded into the cramped quarters of the Operations Office in anticipation to learn what I had to say. Some chose to stand against a wall others took a slumped pose on the floor. As I walked in I said my hellos and thanked them for making themselves available to me, I didn't waste any time. I got right to the point. I said I don't know how many of you have seen the list of nonconformities we received from our client recently, or what efforts have been taken to address them. Immediately one team member said "what list" and another said "if you're talking about why we're closing down…no one has told us anything other than we really f----- up." And another said "yea, we asked but no one would tell us anything…they just said we screwed up and now our days are numbered…are we going to lose our jobs or what."

Wow…what an eye opener…I wasn't expecting that! It quickly became obvious that no one had bothered to provide them any insight into what had occurred regarding the nonconformities or made any effort to address them. So, the first thing I did was read off the list of nonconformities one-by-one. As I did something interesting began to happen. Those that were slumped up against the wall began to sit up and some even stood. They said things like "what…we can fix that…" and "that's a no brainer…why didn't we get a chance to fix that…" and some expressed denials and questioned the accuracy and even existence of some of the nonconformities.

After making it through the entire list I told them that I knew we didn't have a lot of time right now to discuss each nonconformity, but that I would like to have them help me prioritize the list by those that they believed could be addressed quickly versus those that would require a bit more time and effort. It only took us another 20 minutes or so to accomplish this before I decided to turn them loose. When I looked up at the clock, I realized that we had talked almost on up into the lunch hour. The lunch horn would be sounding in just 35 minutes so I asked if they would be willing to continue our discussion through lunch, if I ordered some pizza. All agreed but one—the Custodian who also happened to be the Shop Steward for the group. He quickly broke into a lecture about how it would be against their Union Contract if they had to work through lunch without reasonable prior notification and agreed to pay them time and a half…or something to that affect. Before I could respond everyone in the room began to talk over him and demanded that he sit down and shut up. As he was clearly outnumbered, he simply shrugged, but didn't sit down. I stopped just long enough to order some pizzas and soda and we picked up where I left off. By the time the pizza arrived we even narrowed the list down to what we called the "Top Ten." It was comprised of the most major of nonconformities that had plagued the operation for more than a year and cost the company (and the client) dearly. By the time the pizza and sodas were gone…we had a game plan and I had their commitment. It was a risk but I told them that if they collaborated with me and each other, I would make sure that their jobs were secure and the account would stay or I would resign my position. Their drive and self-confidence reinforced my own confidence that I could deliver on this promise.

Over the days and weeks that followed, we looked at each key function within the warehouse operation and the tasks supporting them. We evaluated the value of each task and eliminated those tasks deemed to have no value. Those tasks that remained, we ensured they were governed by current work instructions and that the owners of each task or those impacted by process changes were properly educated and trained. Nonconformities identified per the prior external audit were ticked off one by one until we had successfully addressed them all. All of our efforts were accomplished through team collaboration and without any [recorded] overtime. Overall production was up to boot.

As word got out in our organization and to the client, management from other departments and locations stopped by unannounced to tour our facility to witness firsthand what we had claimed to have accomplished. Then we received a call from a regional manager representing our client who provided a heads up that an "audit" was going to take place sometime within the next couple of days. While upper management was catapulted into the panic mode, I remained confident that the audit would work in our favor…what better way to get the client into our facility to see firsthand what we had accomplished?

The audit consisted of one guy, but not just any guy. He was notoriously known as the toughest auditor and the senior representative within their internal quality group. It was rumored that he invented auditing and that he was so tough and thorough that he shows up [literally] with a White glove to check for any accumulation of dust on racking units and product cartons. I couldn't have been prouder when I asked for volunteers to stay to help prepare for the audit—off the clock—and they all stepped forward—even the Shop Steward. We didn't take any chances so it was an all out "dusting" event that kept us all in the warehouse until the wee hours of the night.

My Father would refer to it as "assholes and elbows time." For some reason over the years when he used this phrase to kick-off Saturday morning cleaning events in our home as kids, I always found it funny. That is until the reality of the event set in and we found ourselves on our hands and knees and our behinds pointing upward as we cleaned the underneath of our beds, scrubbed floors, pulled weeds in the yard and edged the sidewalk with hand clippers.

That night prior to the audit…I will always remember my team and the dedication that spilled over into their efforts. You couldn't ask for a better example of true team work in action. They were great. The following morning around 07:30 the auditor of all auditors showed up and I'll be dammed if he didn't have a White glove hanging out of his back pocket…I suspect…for all to see…as a fear factor I'm sure. We introduced ourselves and as I proceeded to offer him a cup of coffee, orange juice or whatever we had…his reply was "no—let's just get this thing started…why don't you just show me to your warehouse…"

As we walked from the front lobby, into the administrative area and through the door leading to the warehouse floor, he stopped rather suddenly, when he saw the organizational chart we had created a few weeks ago using life-size individual head shots of our team members accompanied with a brief description of their team role. He never said anything but took plenty of time to examine the pictures and read each caption below them. When he finished the last one, he just turned towards the warehouse and headed off into the isles with me close behind. He (I believe) intentionally walked to the rear of the warehouse before turning into an isle probably assuming we spent most of our effort making the front isles ready for his visit neglecting those towards the rear of the warehouse. That wasn't the case; we gave the same level of attention to all the isles. As he requested, we walked up and then down each isle so that he could view both sides and all the racks, every few sections he reached out to brush the palm of his hand (minus the White glove) across the top of a carton and then turning his hand over to see if any accumulation of dust appeared. I'm sure he was somewhat disappointed—as a result of our thorough cleaning job the night before.

Further into the audit, he happened to look up to one of the top racks and noticed a carton that appeared to be damaged. This seemed to please him…the fact that he actually found something of concern. He turned to me and asked why the carton remained in inventory when it was damaged. I informed him that it would be discovered when the "isle owner" conducted their morning isle inspection. When he asked what that consisted of, I walked him to the end of the isle where a photo was mounted under the words "This Isle is Mine." I explained that every isle is assigned to someone who is responsible to facilitate what I call a "FOD Walk" a term I borrowed from my days as a Crew Chief on the flight line at George Air Force Base back in the late 70's. FOD being an acronym for Foreign Object Damage. I explained that each morning the isle owner did a physical and visual sweep of his isle to look for debris (broken pallet pieces, stretch wrap, etc.), empty pallets left in the racks, spills and damaged product. The auditor of all auditors wanted to challenge this process and insisted on waiting until the isle owner made their sweep of this particular isle—just to see if they noticed the damaged product and if they actually removed it from its place on the top rack. As we stood off to the side it didn't take long before the isle owner appeared to perform his FOD Walk and I was extremely relieved to see him come to a stop below the damaged carton, visually note its location, leave to retrieve a lift truck, return, raise himself up and remove the damaged carton. As he did, the auditor quickly walked over and asked how he knew the damaged carton existed. The isle owner, without hesitation said he found it as part of his FOD Walk. The auditor then requested that we observe the process of what the isle owner does once they retrieved the damaged carton—which we did without the auditor noting any nonconformities or observations. That was probably due to the fact that two weeks prior, we completed the update of our SOPs which included the new one for this process.

By the time the auditor had concluded his thorough audit of the operation, he could not identify a single nonconformity to report and only offered some minor observations—which were quickly addressed prior to his departure. Needless to say, we received our first ever 100% quality audit—the first of three in a row that we would receive before my role changed in the organization when I was asked to head up our first Quality Group dedicated to quality assurance and continuous improvement. Oh, and as far as our probationary period with the client… it came to an end when the client decided to renew our contract…for three more years…

As a direct result of this experience, *Getting Business Fit* was born. I moved on to apply the "fit" approach in all future endeavors with continual success in improving work processes and eliminating waste in various business industries to the tune of millions in bottom line savings.

Gary King

Okay, enough about my past successes, let's work on making yours one to talk about.

Step 1 – Task Analysis

Everything is perfect within our organization, even our desire to improve it. —Gary King

First things first being educate yourself, how well do you believe you know your organization? I'm not just referring to your vision, mission, products, services, or operating locations, I'm referring to your business process, functions and the tasks that are completed day in and day out. Do you see them as perfect…or good enough or do you know that they are perfect? Remember, when it comes to continual improvement and best practices…the process is never complete—it's never ending. What about the individuals who carry out those tasks—how well do you know them and how well do they know you? Are they putting forth their best effort? Are you? What about your customers, do you know what they want and need today and tomorrow? Do you know what they think of you, your organization and the products or services you provide them? When was last time you flat out asked them? If it hasn't been at least six months ago… be concerned…be very concerned. Things are happening extremely fast these days and customer loyalty is the only guarantee that can assure your future success.

"One sees great things from the valley, only small things from the peak." —G.K. Chesterton

Most executives tend to view things from a higher peak which has them far removed from the day-to-day workings of what occurs in the valleys. After all, you have senior managers, mid-managers and supervisors that oversee the various levels of work. Maybe the better question is how much of your organization do you "need" to see? One could spend a majority of their career trying to figure the answer to that one out. But, as your time is valuable I'll just jump you right to the answer… you need to know and see *enough*. Okay, not fair…how much is enough? By the time you've made it through the business fit process you will know and have seen more of your organization than just enough. And so will your leadership team and workforce.

Define Your Organization

To begin the process first we must define your organization. This will be accomplished as I take you through a Task Analysis. It may seem tedious and time consuming at the start but once you begin the process you'll get through it rather quickly and soon recognize the many learnings and benefits that will result.

We'll begin the task analysis by creating a simple Excel spreadsheet containing the following headers: *Function, Task, Task Owner, Hourly Rate, Backup Owner, Work Type, Customer, Task Frequency, Hours, Annual Cost, Formal Training, and Work Instructions/SOPs.* As you progress through the task analysis, you may choose to add additional headers that better represent your business. Once your spreadsheet has been created, you're ready to begin the next step in your education—identifying with your Functions.

Identifying With Your Work Functions

As we continue with the Task Analysis process you will now begin populating your task analysis spreadsheet. Under the "Function" header, list all the functions that make up your organization e.g., product development, planning, forecasting, purchasing, sourcing, selling, marketing, manufacturing, designing, shipping, receiving, distribution, transportation, maintenance, accounts payable/receivable, customer satisfaction, etc., etc.—every function no matter how large or small—list them all. You can begin by taking a stab at listing them all yourself or just jump right to a workout session with your leadership team. It might be a good exercise for you to try and identifying as many work functions you can recall, before soliciting the help of your leadership team to ensure that you capture every work function no matter how large or small or how frequent or infrequent the function is performed.

Additional functions that are usually overlooked that generate a lot of waste include: Meetings, Conference Calls, Reports, Travel and Entertainment, Contracts, and Utilities. Be sure to include these functions as part of your task analysis. This might be a good time to share another short story with you regarding hidden waste in forgotten functions such as those listed above.

My "Other" Story

"We must not, in trying to think about how we can make a big difference, ignore the small daily differences we can make which, over time, add up to big differences that we often cannot foresee." —Marian Wright Edelman

A few years ago in an effort to increase productivity and eliminate waste, I was facilitating a Task Analysis for a major account. Although they had a reputation for having too many meetings what we discovered as part of the brainstorming process—most would find unbelievable. I assure you what I'm about to share with you is true—it really did happen.

During our process of listing all current reports with the goal of reducing their content, frequency, distribution, or eliminate them all together, we came across one in particular that seemed to impact everyone present. It required at least two hours of daily input and one hour review from each of the twenty managers and their admin staff that represents four separate locations. The report was initiated by an executive representing our client a year and a half prior and distributed to five additional client executives ever since. It looked like it had potential so we decided to investigate. We tried to locate and contact the originator of the year and a half old report only to learn that he had retired a year earlier. We then reached out to the five original client executives on the reports distribution list. One by one they confirmed that they received copies of the report but since it really didn't pertain to their business group, they just electronically filed it away. Further investigation into the purpose and intent of the report revealed that it was initiated as a corrective action to a major quality incident that had occurred back when the report was first generated over a year and a half ago. The report was to run for at least 90-days to monitor a change in a key process to ensure that the quality incident would not reoccur. No one could recall a single reoccurrence but the report never went away. The initiator retired and like clockwork the report continued to live on as just something we were told we had to generate everyday and email off to the five client executives.

That report, the one we're talking about…guess how much it cost us to produce? Or, I should say cost out client, being a cost-plus operation.

Let's do some quick [conservative] calculations—

- 20 Managers at an hourly rate of $50 = $1,000

- 8 Admins at an hourly rate of $25

- 20 Managers x 3 hours per day x 5 days x 52 weeks = $780,000

- 8 Admins x 1 hour per day x 5 days x 52 weeks = $52,000

- Per 18 months = **$1.248 Million**

It quickly became known as the "Million Dollar Report" and was eliminated. And this was just one example…we found many more…some originating from the client, others originating from us. Shame on them, but more shame on us, we were supposed to be the 3PL experts. We also went on to reduce and eliminate several meeting requirements (face-to-face and conference calls) which in turn reduced travel and entertainment costs. We looked at existing service contracts that we were able to renegotiate and even found ways to conserve energy that lead to substantial savings in Utilities. So, again don't underestimate these forgotten functions…they can be a major contributor of waste and non-value work. Don't ignore the small daily differences we can make…

Task Your Functions

Each function is comprised of a series of steps or tasks that must be completed to satisfy the requirements of a process or work function. For example, let's take a typical receiving function where tasks might include:

- Advanced shipment notification (ASN) received,
- Security notified of pending delivery,
- Receiving personnel scheduled,
- Trailer inspected at security (condition of/seal intact),
- Trailer assigned to dock door,
- Trailer secured at dock door,
- Trailer unloaded to manifest,
- Product scanned in,
- Product staged, and
- Product put-a-way or cross-docked for outbound shipment.

Depending on the industry you serve, your functions and work tasks can vary a great deal. Moving to the right on your task analysis spreadsheet and under the header *Tasks*, begin listing all the tasks that are required within each of your work functions.

FUNCTION	TASK	TASK OWNER	BACKUP OWNER	HOURLY RATE	WORK TYPE	CUSTOMER
Receiving	ASN Received					
"	Security Notified					
"	Receiver Scheduled					

Example – *Task Analysis Spreadsheet w/Tasks*

Don't overly concern yourself with having to recall them all at this stage of the task analysis…just try to recall the more obvious ones. Later on when you facilitate this process with your leadership team, you can pick up where you left off and capture all remaining [known] tasks. What they cannot recall, your task experts can and will further on in your task analysis when you brainstorm with them.

Assign Ownership to Tasks

It is imperative that each task have an identified owner. These owners are comprised of the individuals that perform the tasks day in and day out. They are the experts and you need to view them as such. In your task analysis spreadsheet under the header "Owner" list the employee(s) or the job title assigned to perform each task listed. This is where you definitely need to incorporate the help of your leadership team and if necessary a representative from Human Resources. This information is essential to have and will help determine the participants of your upcoming brainstorming sessions. If the task is performed by one to three individuals, list their names. If performed by four or more, note the job title and number of individuals performing the task. Example: Jim and Diane are your Receiving Clerks who work for the receiving function. So, under task owner you will list Jim / Diane. If there are four or more assigned Receiving Clerks, instead of listing their names you would simply enter Receiving Clerks: 4, 5 or however many are normally assigned.

TASK OWNER	BACKUP OWNER	HOURLY RATE	WORK TYPE	CUSTOMER	CUSTOMER TYPE	TASK FREQ
Jim/Diane	Bob	$26	R			
Jim/Diane	Bob	$26	R			
Diane	Bob	$26	R			
Rcvg Clrk: 3	None	$14	R			
Bob	Diane	$26	R			

Example – *Task Analysis Spreadsheet w/Owners*

Assign Backup Ownerships to Tasks

All work tasks must have a properly trained backup owner identified who has been evaluated to ensure they are capable of performing those tasks they back up when and if they are needed. They should periodically perform the tasks they back up to remain proficient and at the ready. This will ensure that work functions continue to flow without interruption or downtime during peak times or the absence of resources. This will also reduce or eliminate the need to bring in Agency "Temps" or accrue costly overtime. No matter how efficient your leadership team may be, when the going gets tough and quick decisions are needed, if you don't have adequate resources—including qualified back-ups, you leave your leaders with few options but to call in temps or approve overtime. If backups have not been assigned for each task, for now, list those that have and we will revisit this column when you brainstorm with the experts.

Determine Hourly Rates

Once we get further into the task analysis and begin identifying tasks for possible elimination, you're going to want to know what potential savings will result. Completing this process will help you associate hourly value or "costs" to existing tasks. Below is a simple process that will help you calculate a usable hourly rate with benefits, even if you have multiple workers performing the same task. I have used this for years and it has stood up to the scrutiny of many a financial gurus. To determine a task owner's [loaded] rate begin by identifying their hourly pay rate as demonstrated below.

- Jim is at an hourly pay rate of **$20**
- Diane is at an hourly pay rate of **$21**
- Bob is at an hourly pay rate of **$18**

When multiple workers perform the same task, you'll want to average their hourly rate. Noting the hourly rate of the Receiving Clerks above, the averaged hourly pay rate would be: $19.66 rounded up to $20 per hour.

Now, multiply 2080 (hours in a year based on a 40 hour work week) times $20 (averaged hourly rate) which should equal: $41,600.

$$2080 \times \$20 = \$41{,}600$$

Add at least 30% for benefits (or whatever rate you currently use) which brings our loaded total up to: $54,080.

$$\$41{,}600 + 30\% = \$54{,}080$$

Finally, divide the loaded total ($54,080) by 2080 and you end up with the adjusted and loaded hourly rate of $26 that you'll want to use in costing tasks performed by these individuals.

$$\$54{,}080 / 2080 = \$26$$

Use the same approach when calculating and averaging the hourly rate where four or more owners are assigned to the same task.

Define Your Work and Waste

Now we're starting to get into the meat and potatoes of the task analysis—as this is a crucial step in identifying, quantifying and eliminating waste in your organization. But first we need to have a clear understanding on how we work and the many forms of waste that we create within our work. Let's begin by looking at the definition of work and waste that I work by, as defined by William E. Conway of Conway Management Company…another great Quality Mentor of mine.

Mr. Conway defines Work as:

"…a set of tasks performed by people, machines,

energy, computers, chemical processes, water, air, etc. to meet an objective, measured by the time taken, its cost and the resulting quality."

Taking from my learnings from Mr. Conway, I too place work types into four categories, they are:

1. *Value Work (V):* This is work defined by the customer as adding or having value from the perspective of what they want or need at any given time. For example, a customer might want a purse to go with their dress, a tie to go with a suit, or a drink to go with their meal. And, they might need a tax consultant for their business, a realtor to sell their home, or like you... customers for their products. Work that meets the criteria of satisfying the customer's wants and needs is therefore viewed by the customer as work that they are willing to pay for.

2. *Required Work (R):* Required Work is work that may not provide direct value from the customer's perspective but is essential or required of your business process. For example: paying your bills and taxes, processing payroll, processing expense reports, etc... Your customer may not benefit from this work but I'm sure you would agree that you would be hard pressed to service your customer efficiently (or remain in business) without accomplishing required work.

3. *Non-Value Work (NV):* Non-value work is work that provides no value from the customer's perspective or is not required to run your business. A primary example of non-value work is work that begins with "Re" such as Recoup, Rework, Reship, Returns,

Repack, Replace, etc. It's usually associated with having to handle product or services more than once, which means after the first time, every second, third, fourth attempt at the work is at an unplanned cost and therefore an ultimate loss to your bottom-line. It also includes work that has evolved over time to accommodate short-cuts or to avoid less desirable work tasks. An abundance of improvement opportunities exist within non-value work tasks which is why you'll want to allocate a majority of your time seeking out improvement opportunities, once you've completed your task analysis process.

4. **Non-Work (N):** Non-work would be just that... having no work to do or work not getting done. Having no work might result from poor planning, bottle necks, etc., while work not getting done can result from the absence of human resources— planned or unplanned, and when equipment is down or unavailable. This type of work should be reduced and whenever feasible eliminated along with non-value work.

Waste

Waste goes beyond the obvious such as material scrap...way beyond. Unfortunately many have yet to figure this out...or remain in denial that waste exists within their organization.

Mr. Conway defines Waste as:

"...the difference between the way things are now and

the way they could or should be if everything were right—no troubles, problems, errors, or complexities."

He further narrows waste down to four forms.

Waste of—material, time, capital and gross profit (lost sales/lost opportunities) and emphasizes that the biggest waste of all is lost sales, lost gross margin, and lost opportunities.

Mr. Conway suggests five basic ways to search for waste:

1. Follow the market (external customer), competition, technology
2. Follow money – P&L, sales, cost of quality
3. Follow systems, processes
4. Follow people
5. Follow time

In searching for waste we must look at our business from a different perspective or through a different lens—as Mr. Conway puts it…allowing us to identify more potential opportunities to improve processes and eliminate waste.

For more information regarding work and waste, I highly recommend that you secure a copy of one of my favorite books that I personally use as a resource in defining work and waste—*The Quality Secret: The Right Way to Manager* by William E. Conway, Conway Management Company, Inc.

Contact information:

Conway Management Company, Inc.

15 Trafalgar Square
Nashua, New Hampshire 03063 USA
603.889.1130 – 800.359.0099
Fax: 603.889.0033
www.conwaymgmt.com

They also have additional publications that I have found to be extremely helpful when facilitating a task analysis such as *"Waste Chasers, a Pocket Companion to Quality and Productivity."*

Define Your Customers

Customers are your bread and butter—without them there is no business. It is essential that you know who they are and what they want, need and expect of your products and services. You need to clearly hear the Voice of the Customer (VOC) and listen to what they say and perceive about the quality of service and products you provide. Notice I said "perceive"—as perception rules the day. It doesn't matter if you know one thing as a matter of fact, if the customer's perception is that of another. Now, let's take a look at how we define your customers.

Customers fall into one of two categories: Internal and External. The internal customers are those individuals in your organization that rely on the work of others within your organization to complete their work. For example: If you're a manager and you have a position that reports to you that has become vacant, you will be requiring the services and support of Human Resources (HR) to help recruit for a replacement. As such you are now an internal customer of HR until a replacement candidate has been found, interviewed, and successfully hired.

The external customer usually exists outside the walls of your organization. They purchase the products you produce or services your organization provides. Next to each work task and under the header "Customer" list those customers of the work task and whether they are an internal or external customer. Use an "I" to represent internal customers and an "X" to represent external customers.

CUSTOMER	CUSTOMER TYPE	TASK FREQ	HOURS	FORMAL TRAINING	SOPs WIs	ANNUAL COST
Operations	I					
Joe Public	X					

This information will be most useful once you've identified tasks for possible elimination and you set out to educate those that will be impacted by the change. If you have multiple customers for a particular task, be sure to list them all. For the sake of limited space within your excel spreadsheet cells, you may want to reference a separate document or worksheet where you can create a detailed list of the multiple customers.

Determine Task Frequency and Hours

The amount of frequency that each task is performed is crucial in determining the cost of each task. As you consider each task, determine if they are performed daily, weekly, monthly, quarterly, annually, or any other frequency that you measure by and use your best estimate as to how many hours within each frequency are committed to performing each task. Later in the exercise you will see how we use this information. It's important that you set aside adequate time to determine how often each task is performed and the amount of hours associated with each frequency. This step will be revisited and "fine tuned" as part of the brainstorming process with your task experts. So at this stage, just list the frequency and hours as you know or expect them to be.

TASK FREQ	HOURS	FORMAL TRAINING	SOPs WIs	ANNUAL COST
Daily	2			
Weekly	4			

Prepare Your Workforce

"You start with good people, you train and motivate them, you give them an opportunity to advance—then the organization succeeds." —J. W. "Bill" Marriott, Jr. Chairman and CEO, Marriot International, Inc.

How able is your leadership team to consistently lead effectively and your workforce to consistently perform their assigned tasks efficiently? Do they have the adequate resources, tools and proper skills to succeed? Do you provide formalized training to ensure work objectives are met and that ultimately work processes become best practices? Don't allow a "No" response to keep you from moving forward. You can always revisit this within *Step*

1 Task Analysis, Brainstorm with the Experts. For now, we just need to determine if formal (documented) training for each task is provided, so, under the header "Training" simply enter a "Y" for yes and "N" for no.

FORMAL TRAINING	SOPs WIs	ANNUAL COST
N		
N		

Govern Your Workforce

You'll want to verify if controlled work instructions or standard operating procedures exist for each work task. Many organizations make the mistake of neglecting this important requirement. Either they don't bother taking the time to develop the written documents or they do but only to the point of storing them in a binder on a shelf where they only come out as part of an internal audit review. Work instructions or standard operating procedures should be the document that is used to train a task owner to perform their assigned task correctly each and every time and to hold them accountable accordingly. If the process has changed or been improved, this document serves as the record to track the changes and ensure that going forward, the new process is adhered to. If current work instructions or standard operating procedures are in place for the task noted, under the header "SOPs/WIs" enter a "Y" for yes and if not an "N" for no.

SOPs WIs	ANNUAL COST
N	
N	

Costing Your Tasks

"You don't get paid for the hour. You get paid for the value you bring to the hour." —Jim Rohn

When you seek to eliminate or at least reduce tasks identified as *Non-Value Work* or *Non-work*, you'll want to know their cost so you can calculate your anticipated savings. Depending on the amount of projected savings, this calculation will help you and your team members prioritize which tasks might be eliminated first, second, third and so on—especially if team resources are stretched. Using a calculation within Excel, extend the cost per task so that it appears in the cell below the header *Annual Cost*.

CUSTOMER	CUSTOMER TYPE	TASK FREQ	HOURS	FORMAL TRAINING	SOPs WIs	ANNUAL COST
Operations	I	Daily	2	N	N	$27,040
Joe Public	X	Weekly	4	N	N	$2,912

Task Owners x Hourly Rate x Frequency x Hours = Annual Cost

2 (task owners) x $26 (hourly rate) = $52

2 hours per day (frequency) x $52 = $104 per day

5 days per week x $104 = $520 per week

52 weeks x $520 = $27,040 (annual cost to perform this task(s))

Brainstorm with the Experts

"We know where most of the creativity, the innovation, the stuff that drives productivity lies – in the minds of those closest to the work. –Jack Welch

This is my favorite step in the process of getting business fit and will soon become yours I'm sure. This is where the improvement process comes together and where all the magic happens. I assure you this step will be a true wake up call for you and the brainstorming participants. It will also be an excellent opportunity for you to interact with your leadership team and workforce while receiving an education on how your organization really functions. Just keep in mind that your ultimate goal is to identify non-value work that can be eliminated…and your objective—to identify all tasks within your key work processes—especially the hidden ones. You are seeking out improvement opportunities that will deliver substantial savings so that you can transition task owners of non-value work being eliminated—over to value work as part of the "business fitting" process.

Amnesty as Opposed to Blame, Fear and Reprisal

Tasks that give refuge to hidden waste are those born out of individuals taking short cuts or cutting corners. But these hidden tasks may also consist of work that has led to undocumented process improvement. You must put forth the effort to identify all tasks known, hidden or otherwise before you can decipher which should be eliminated, reduced or potentially embraced as best practices. That is why it is extremely crucial when going into the brainstorming session that you instill a sense of amnesty for all who bring forward tasks—no matter what value they may or may not provide within a work process. There is NO PLACE for criticism, fear of reprisal or retaliation for those that step up and expose the fact that they may have created short cuts or cut corners and therefore jeopardized the quality of product or service output. The only logical way to expose the hidden tasks is if you instill assurances to all participants that our goal is to identify opportunities for improvements, not to allocate blame. Your measure of sincerity in getting this across to your participants will dictate the measure to which you are able to identify and eliminate a substantial amount of hidden waste.

Brainstorming in itself can be a fun and challenging exercise for all who participate in the process. It also serves as a great way to get everyone engaged in positive and rewarding change. It will empower participants to play a key role in achieving substantial organizational improvements.

Task Analysis Spreadsheet

At this point, let's make some minor adjustments to the appearance of your task analysis spreadsheet. Bring up the electronic version of your existing task analysis spreadsheet and sort the data by the "function column" to reflect the order in which the functions in your organization flow. A simple way to accomplish this is to first go down your list of functions and number them in the order that they occur then sort the numbers in ascending order. Numbering them in the natural order that the work flows will also help you and your employees visualize the flow in order to easily identify additional tasks that may have been missed in your first pass.

Protecting Confidentiality of Hourly Rates

You can choose to "hide" the column that lists the hourly rate for the task owners—if this information is considered confidential. However, the most powerful aspect of this exercise is in discovering and revealing the true cost associated with performing tasks and educating your workforce accordingly. These costs will serve as a powerful tool in securing the support of your employees when tying costs to work tasks that do not add value and therefore may be marked for elimination.

A suggestion might be to simply hide the "frequency" column—which would make it nearly impossible to guess an individual's hourly rate. Again, it all depends on how much information you're prepared to share with your brainstorming participants.

Reproducing the Task Analysis Spreadsheet

If you have the capability in-house to produce a large printed version of your spreadsheet via a plotter, or access to a local print shop that can reproduce it for you, please do so…the larger the better. I like to enlarge mine to at least the size of an average flip chart pad turned on its side. In addition to the enlarged version of your spreadsheets, you'll want to reproduce a large version of the definitions of Work and Waste. I would further suggest that you provide reduced sized copies as handouts for your brainstorming participants, in advance of the scheduled brainstorming session for them to preview and better prepare.

Preliminary Instructions in Preparation for the Brainstorming Session

When providing an advanced copy of the task analysis spreadsheet and definitions of Work and Waste to your brainstorming participants, be sure to include some preliminary instructions to help them prepare for the brainstorming session. The instructions should instruct them to review:

- All functions listed thus far and make note of any that may have been omitted.

- All work tasks listed within their assigned function and note any that may have been omitted.

- All task owners and backup owners listed and note any that are incorrect or have been omitted.

- All Customers listed and note any that are outdated or have been omitted.

- The frequencies listed for each task and note any inaccuracies.

- The hours listed to complete each task per frequency and note any inaccuracies.

- The Y and N responses listed per the existence of formal training. Does it exist and is it actually planned and facilitated?

- The Y and N response listed per the existence of <u>current</u> work instructions and standard operating procedures for accuracy. Do they exist; are they current and easily accessible?

Schedule the Brainstorming Session

Set a date and time for the first introductory brainstorming session but not too far out from when participants have been provided the preliminary instructions. I would suggest that you schedule your session no more than a week out from when your preliminary instructions are received by your intended participants. As a personal preference I further suggest that you schedule your first session at around 08:30 on a

Wednesday morning. I have found that participants are generally at their peak by the morning of mid-week. Of course, this may depend on the need to facilitate multiple sessions to accommodate a larger workforce or multiple shifts. I prefer Wednesday mornings also because it's smack in the middle of the work week providing a couple of days before the session and a couple of days after. This allows for last minute preparation, promotion of the session to drum up interest leading up to it, and gives folks plenty of time to shake off the wild weekend they just had. Having a few days following the session allows for quick follow up actions to occur as needed.

Prepare your Leadership Team

Before this first brainstorming session, reach out to all your leadership personnel to educate them on what you've learned so far from this book. You'll want to make sure that your leadership team "gets it" and is onboard. Having only one dissenter will ensure your efforts will suffer as they work behind the scenes to undermine them. It must be an all or nothing proposition with all heads nodding in the same direction. And, you <u>cannot</u> waiver on your own commitment in seeing this through. Your workforce will look to you and your leaders as the example. They will determine their level of commitment based on their <u>perception</u> of yours and members of your leadership team. Coach your leaders to be active participants and obvious supporters of the brainstorming session. No ideas are bad ideas, no personal attacks, and no negative connotations.

Select and Prepare Your Session Facilitator

Assign an owner to help prepare for and facilitate the brainstorming sessions. Reserve a conference room that will accommodate the number of participants planned; ensure that all equipment and supplies are on hand (See the Brainstorming Tool Kit below); have the enlarged spreadsheet pages that you had reproduced mounted where they can be viewed from all sitting areas in the conference room; and promote the heck out of the session leading up to it—generating excitement and anticipation.

When scheduling your brainstorming session(s) depending on the number of participants and factors such as multiple work shifts, floor coverage, etc., you may have to schedule multiple sessions.

It's always best to retain the services of a professional facilitator but if time and your budget cannot accommodate, then the first choice should be you—the person at the top. Outside of a professional facilitator, you can't find a better way to gain support and participation and to let your people know how important the sessions are than to have you lead them and (at the least) directly participate in them. If facilitating is not your bag, select a leader within your organization that has already earned the respect of their peers and workforce. Make sure the individual you choose completely understands and supports your vision of getting business fit and possess the appropriate skill sets to facilitate, before allowing them to commit to the facilitator's role.

Brainstorming Tool Kit

#	ITEM	QTY	NOTES
1	Equipment (laptop, VCR, Monitor, Overhead Projector, Screen, etc.	As needed	Make sure they are all operating properly before the start of the session.
2	Flip Charts	At least two, more if needed	I prefer the Post-it-Note version for ease of mounting on walls.
3	Markers (large)	At least four different collors and a set for each flip chart used.	I prefer the Post-it-Note brand for ease of mounting on walls.
4	Post-it-Notes	At least a packet for each participant	If possible, secure a unique color for each Function being worked.
5	Pens	At least one for each participant	Preferably Black ink and easy to handle
6	Masking Tape	At least one (one inch width) role	Use this for those stubborn walls/surfaces that might reject the Post-it-Note adhesive backing.
7	Transparencies	As required	Only if you still prefer the use of an overhead projector.
8	Laser Pointer	At least one	I like to use them whenever I'm presenting or facilitating a session.
9	Water	At least two each for each participant	You will also want to make arrangements for additional refreshments to accommodate the length of time spent in each session. This may include ordering in lunch. Make sure someone owns this task.
10	Candy	A couple of bags	Little hard candy mints help screen the coffee breath and relax the participants between meals.
11	Comfortable Working Environment	As needed	You want the participants to feel physically and emotionally relaxed for peak participation.
12	Start Time	As determined	You'll want to establish some ground rules with one of them being that meetings will begin on time, even if all the participants are not there.
13	Warm-up Activity	At least one	To help break the ice and loosen things up a bit, you'll want to facilitate a simple (fun) warm up activity or at least tell a humorous story about yourself. Humor goes a long way to putting folks at ease.
14	Ground Rules	As determined	Have them prepared in advance and provide a handout of them to all participants before reviewing each of them with them.
15	Agenda	As determined	Have one complete with time allocated for each agenda topic.
16	Minutes	As needed	Assign an owner to take minutes for the session and to distribute them within a timely manner following each completed session.
17	Schedule	As defined	Assign a time keeper to ensure the agenda and times set aside for each topic are followed. Keep to the schedule.
18	Guidelines	As defined	To ensure effective discussions and conflict resolution.
19	Parking Lot	As defined	For items to be discussed at another time.
20	Wrap-up	As defined	To assign responsibilities, completion dates for future work, and decide on next meeting with tentative agenda.

Also see the Brainstorming Session Preparation Checklist in the Appendix as Exhibit B

Brainstorming Session #1

The first brainstorming session will set the tone for those that will follow so make the best of it. Begin like you would any other meeting with self introductions (unless everyone is already on a first name basis).

The Ice Breaker

No matter how long you and your participants have worked together or have come to know each other, an "icebreaker" to establish a comfortable relaxed environment is in order. I have found it best to incorporate some humor into a personal story that relates to the purpose for this gathering. Maybe a reference to how you yourself had contributed to non-value work or waste only learning of it once you committed to getting business fit—while incorporating a bit of humor to laugh at yourself. An example might be how you were scheduling daily meetings requiring all leadership personnel to attend—only to learn that a meeting once per week with fewer participants would more than suffice at an annual savings of e.g. *$25,000*. A great way to demonstrate to your participants that no one is infallible when it comes to contributing to non-value work and waste—not even you.

Your story should serve as a relaxed start before getting into the purpose and intent of this first brainstorming session. The relaxed rapport will encourage a greater degree of individual and group participation earlier in the session—allowing more learning to be accomplished and information to be captured. Time permitting—prearrange for one of your leaders to share a similar experience where they may have unwittingly contributed to waste. Better yet, open it up to the participants to share their experiences—all great ways to break the ice and get the session off to a good start.

Brainstorming Overview

Now that you successfully maneuvered beyond the icebergs, you'll want to provide an overview of the purpose and intent of the first brainstorming session as:

- An opportunity to engage all employees in efforts to identify opportunities for process improvement.

- An exercise in identifying opportunities to transition resources (people) away from non-value wasteful work over to more meaningful value-add work.

- An exercise to empower the "real experts" (those that perform the work tasks), to potentially redefine the organization.

Handouts

You'll want to provide handouts of the task analysis spreadsheet that includes the additional input you previously solicited from your leadership personnel and take some time to review it—bringing everyone up to speed on the captured data. Refer to the enlarged spreadsheet you've had mounted to the wall, moving from left to right through each of the headers. Be sure to thoroughly explain the purpose for each column and the content provided below it—using examples that they can best relate to. Be sure to take some time to review the enlarged definitions of Work and Waste as well.

Group Size

Depending on the size of your first group and make up by functions represented, the approach you take to lead off the session may differ. When considering the size of the group I have always found it best to try and limit it to about a dozen participants per session. I have succeeded with much larger groups as well as a group as few as three, however, they can both be challenging for various reasons. The larger numbers can get you a greater degree of input but challenge you in capturing it all. A smaller group is less likely to present itself as individuals especially if one of the participants has a stronger personality that easily sways the opinion of the others. Some additional advantages and disadvantages to consider in addressing a single function group versus a multi-function group are as follows:

Single Function Group

Advantage: Participants all represent the same work function so they focus on what they know and do best. They can easily identify tasks that may have been omitted from the initial spreadsheet and help close the gap between estimated and actual task frequencies and the hours allocated to each frequency.

Disadvantage: Participants representing the same work function may have a narrowed or biased focus in assessing their own work tasks. This approach does little to promote cross-functional participation. Some of the most valued input on a given function or task has come from individuals outside the function being discussed.

Multiple Functions Group

Advantage: Promotes cross-functional participation. Some of the most valued input on a given function or task has come from individuals outside the function being discussed. Helps educate participants on other organizational functions. This approach can help reduce and even eliminate the "silo effect" that may exist in your organization.

Disadvantage: More or longer sessions may be required. When discussing one function over another, some participants may lose interest when not addressing their own particular function.

If addressing a multi-function group, for the sake of time, it's best that the facilitator choose which function to begin with. Of course, with a single function group you only have one option.

Identify all Tasks (formal or hidden)

If you haven't already, pepper the conference table(s) with the index card sized post-it-notes and markers. Using the post-it-notes, have the participants begin writing down any task within the function being addressed, that are <u>not</u> listed on the spreadsheet. While they are doing this, take a sheet of the Flip Chart and write the name of the function at the top with a large marker and place the sheet up on the wall where it can be easily viewed and reached. As they identify additional tasks with their post-it-notes, have them place them on the corresponding flip chart page. Have them continue to do so until all participants have exhausted any tasks not listed on the spreadsheet.

You will find that over time, the experts will establish their own version of tasks that may streamline processes or result in questionable shortcuts. Unless you have controlled work instructions or standard operating procedures in place that are strictly adhered to, the participants will introduce you and your leadership team to a whole new world that exists in the trenches. How you react to this new world will determine if they will allow you further access into it—or withdraw locking you out of it. It's to your advantage to encourage them to expose their hidden world of uncontrolled tasks. Those uncontrolled tasks may lead to best practices or the ability to eliminate non-value work, increase productivity, prevent errors, reduce damage and defects, enhance customer loyalty... the potential is truly unlimited. Don't blow it! This is where the amnesty we talked about earlier is brought into the session, and fear is locked out.

Identify Task Owners

Moving to the right on your task analysis spreadsheet, have the participants consider the task owners listed on the spreadsheet. Have any been omitted? If so have them write them on a post-it-note and place them on another flip chart page that you will create—that notes the Function at the top followed by a dash and then the words Task Owners. This process continues until you have a consensus that all task owners have been captured.

Identify Backup Task Owners

Have the participants identify any backup owners that may have been omitted from the spreadsheet using a new flip chart page with the Function noted at the top, followed by Backup Owners. This is a great opportunity to also capture the input from the session participants as to potential backup owners for those tasks having none. This process continues until the session participants believe that all backup owners have been captured. You may not have available backups for all identified tasks. This is not unusual but can become a great concern if not addressed sooner rather than later. Make special note of all tasks that still do not have a backup identified at this point. Later, within *Step 4 Educate and Train*, we will address those tasks that are without backup owners.

Identify Customers (Internal & External)

When you get to "Customers" you'll want to be sure to spend some time educating your session participants on the existence of the two customer categories—internal and external. You must emphasize how they both should receive the same level of attention and consideration. (*Refer to Step 1 Task Analysis, Define Your Customers*).

Now help your participants capture any customers that may have been omitted from the spreadsheet thus far—having them write them on a post-it-note and adhere them to another flip chart page that you've labeled with the function being worked and "Customers." For ease of capturing this information after the session, draw a line down the center of the flip chart page—left side for internal customers and the right for external and adhere the post-it-notes accordingly.

Although your external customers tend to be more obvious, it's not unusual to find task owners performing their assigned tasks day in and day out and never knowing who their external customers are. If you don't already, you need to incorporate into your existing new hire orientation and induction process, an introduction to your external customers. This process should take them through a brief overview of each of your external customers and the products produced and services provided to them by your organization. I would even go as far as to recommend that you schedule refresher sessions quarterly providing your workforce updates regarding any changes in external customers and or in the products or services they purchase from your organization or that they sell. I've seen some great companies take the process of educating their workforce about their customers by creating Customer Information Bulletin Boards where they post news articles about their external customers along with statistics like spending trends, etc., and changes within the organization effecting internal customers.

As for your internal customers, this is where most companies really drop the ball. They fail to recognize that internal customers exist too and require the same level of attention and appreciation that is bestowed upon your external customers. Like your external customers, without the existence of your internal customers, your organization could not function. You would lack the necessary resources to produce your products and develop your services. Also like your external customers, you will find task owners performing their assigned tasks day in and day out and never really knowing who their internal customers are. That is why as part of your enhanced new hire orientation and induction process you will include an introduction to your internal customers. This would take them through a brief overview of each of your organization's functions and the products they produce and services they provide. The quarterly refresher sessions would include changes in internal customers and or in the products they produce or services they provide.

However you decide to approach the opportunity of making your workforce aware of and better know their internal and external customers, make sure it doesn't fall victim to those programs that are here today, gone tomorrow, If you're going to do this…do it right, and be prepared to continue doing it indefinitely.

Confirm Task Frequencies

Task frequency may require you to spend a little more time reviewing. How often you and your leadership team assume tasks occur may differ a great deal from how often they <u>really</u> occur. Have a scribe take note of the frequencies of each task as identified by the participating experts.

Hours per Task Frequency

Hours allocated to completing tasks per frequency are another factor that may differ greatly from what you and your leadership team have noted. Again, have a scribe take note of actual hours per frequency as identified by the participating experts.

First Session Wrap-Up

As you bring an end to this first session, begin by thanking the participants for their time and participation. Provide them an overview of the "next steps" to occur and approximately when you will be scheduling them to participate in the next follow up session. Emphasize the value of their input as the task experts and ask that they continue to think about any additional information that may have been omitted from the existing spreadsheet and to pass it on directly to you, your designated facilitator or the designated owner of the spreadsheet.

Cull Captured Session Data

Following the participants departure from the conference room, make sure all flip chart pages and post-it-notes are gathered up and the existing spreadsheet is updated accordingly.

Distribute Captured Session Data

Email an electronic copy of the updated spreadsheet to each of the participants at least 48 hours and preferably within 24 hours—following the session, asking them to review it for any additional input and thanking them again for their continued support and contributions to the task analysis and brainstorming session. If any participants do not have access to a desk top computer, have their immediate supervisors or managers that do… reproduce extra copies and distribute them accordingly.

Preparation for Brainstorming Session #2

In preparation for the next session, be sure to set aside some time for you to review and become very familiar with the definitions of Work and Waste as defined in *Step 1 Task Analysis, Define Your Work and Waste*. Have your leadership team do the same.

Send out a request to all participants asking them to start thinking about their assigned work tasks and which of them they believe add no value or are a complete waste of time. Pose it with…"if you held the keys to the Kingdom, which of the tasks that we've identified thus far would you eliminate?" Provide them with a [sincere] opportunity to expose tasks they view as a waste of time, give their feedback serious attention, and you will find much of the hidden waste that is costing your organization dearly.

Take the same approach we talked about in preparation for your first session, scheduling it and designating a session facilitator. Schedule the next session and invite the same groups(s) of participants.

Brainstorming Session #2

When providing the electronic version of your updated spreadsheet to the session two participants, accompanying it should be some updated instructions to help them prepare for this second session along with a handout defining Work and Waste. Also provide them with the following list of example questions they should consider when evaluating the value of a particular task or work function:

Questions to Ask:

- If your external customer was asked, would they view the task as adding value?

- If your internal customers were asked, would they see value in the task?

- Would eliminating the task negatively impact the process? If so, how?

- Could the task be transitioned to a more appropriate owner or be absorbed within another existing task or process for better efficiency?

- Can the frequency or volume of the task be reduced?

- Can those impacted by the task be reduced?

- Is automation of the task(s) an option?

- Is there time wasted waiting during through put?

- Can work flow or volume be adjusted or workforce varied?

- How can the task(s) be better defined and understood?

The instructions should ask that they bring to the next session, a list of those tasks that they believe to be a complete waste of time or add no value to their work function, and therefore should be considered for elimination.

Review of Tasks for Possible Elimination

Remember, it is imperative to seek out all hidden waste for elimination. So, keep your amnesty promise and check any inkling of retaliation, criticism and fear—at the door

At the start of the second session—after you have welcomed them all back and thanked them for their valued participation in the brainstorming sessions to date, be sure to emphasize the objective of putting it all out on the table and the need for their commitment to help expose any and all potential waste for elimination. Make it clear that it is your desire to eliminate work tasks found to have no value and to transition resources over to more meaningful value-added work.

Put up new flip chart sheets with headers identifying the function(s) the participants represent. Instruct each participant to use the index sized post-it-notes that you again peppered the table with, to write down the task that they have identified for elimination and adhere them to the flip chart sheet representing their function. This should continue until everyone has posted their suggested task(s) for elimination.

Beginning with any of the functions being worked in this session, open dialog to have the participants briefly discuss why each task listed should be eliminated. Be open-minded, and because you briefed them prior to the session, participating leadership personnel should remain open-minded as well. No derogatory remarks, smirks, sighs, rolling of the eyes, etc. should be tolerated. Or again, you will jeopardize the process and risk the chance that the participants will shut down.

Have a scribe take note of each participant's view point in justifying why a particular task should be considered for elimination. Continue with this process encouraging open and candid dialog between the participants. You'll be amazed how much you will learn about what really goes on in your organization. When it begins to wind down and everyone has had an opportunity to address their recommendations start planning your transition over to the next focus area—labeling all tasks by "type of work."

Assigning Type of Work to Tasks

You'll want to spend at least 30 minutes reviewing the definitions of work as defined in *Step 1 Task Analysis, Define Your Work and Waste.* Use specific examples of tasks that are currently listed—those that participants can easily relate to, to demonstrate how tasks fall into one of the four categories of work. Stay away from entering N/A, TBD, unknown, etc. in the cells designated for "type of work." All work tasks must fall into one of the four categories—without exception. Those tasks already identified as non-value by the participants have already been labeled, so begin by entering "NV" in the appropriate "type" cell to the right of each of the non-value tasks.

Referring to the enlarged definitions of Work and Waste, begin the brainstorming process of assigning a work type to each task listed. Only do so if you have adequate time to commit to this exercise. This portion of the session is crucial and therefore must NOT be rushed. If you're running out of time or appear to be "losing the crowd" this is a good breaking point to carry over to the next scheduled session—session number three.

End Session

Again, thank the participants for their participation and inform them that you will be updating the existing spreadsheet to reflect their input from today's session. Immediately following this second session, have the spreadsheet owner update the existing spreadsheet—incorporating the recommendations from session participants. Again, shoot to have the updated task analysis spreadsheet out to the participants within 48 hours, as you'll have a lot of data to cull at this point. Make sure adequate resources have been assigned to ensure the accurate and timely culling and distribution of this data

Follow Up

While session participants wait for the updated spreadsheet, instruct them to take some time to review the remaining tasks not addressed in the prior session(s) if any remain. Instruct them to refer to the work type definitions provided in their handout and enter the work type they believe to be most appropriate. And, instruct them to bring with them—to the next session—their copy of the spreadsheet with their entries for work types noted as a point of reference.

Leadership Team Review

Once the spreadsheet has been updated, email copies to your leadership team with all columns unhidden to show total cost per task and have them carefully review the tasks previously identified by the session participants as non-value, wasteful, or those tasks they would eliminate—given the opportunity to do so.

Schedule a meeting with your leadership team to review each task listed—including those marked for possible elimination. Using the type of work definitions provided in *Step 1 Task Analysis, Define Your Work and Waste*, review each task with your leadership team until everyone is in agreement as to work type for each task listed. Sort the completed spreadsheet first by function and second by work type, so that each task within each function is grouped by work type.

Schedule time with your leadership team to review each task previously identified by session two participants as being non-value and or recommended for elimination. Review all tasks marked as non-value work—closing any gaps between your leadership team and the session two participant's recommendations. If you or your leadership team cannot agree with your session two participant's recommendations, work with them to prepare a simple statement of facts in preparation for the next (third) session. For those tasks where there is agreement for elimination, total their costs as potential savings to share at the next session.

Schedule Brainstorming Session #3

Schedule the next session and invite the same groups(s) of participants from session two.

Brainstorming Session #3

If participants were unable to assign "Work Types" to each task prior to this session due to time constraints, do so now, and once complete, end the session as you did sessions one and two, and schedule a fourth session to accomplish what follows below.

When providing the electronic version of your updated spreadsheet to the session three participants, open the spreadsheet to show the following columns: Function, Task, Task Owner, Work Type, and Total Cost per Task. This third session will be the first time that participants will see costs associated with their functional work tasks and this is usually quite an eye-opener. Be sure to take some time to explain how these costs were calculated (owners averaged hourly rate plus benefits times the hours the task is performed annually).

Open discussions on the tasks that the participants had previously identified as non-value and or those they recommend for elimination. Emphasize all those that the leadership team agreed to before addressing those requiring further discussion. Be sure to emphasize the outstanding effort that has gone into the task analysis process thus far and really play up the potential savings that can result once the tasks identified by THEM, are eliminated.

Have a representative from the leadership team present their explanation as to why certain tasks cannot be eliminated. Be sensitive to the prior recommendations of participants. As an exercise, invite the participants to present their justification for the tasks they've previously recommended for elimination that are in dispute with the views of the leadership team. The tone should be kept positive and dialog encouraged until either the participants agree with the leadership teams' findings our visa versa. If at an impasse, the task in dispute should be placed in the "Parking Lot" and set aside for further review at a later date. But, I have yet to arrive at an impasse between participants and leadership personnel at this stage of the process. Justifications to or not to eliminate a particular task at this point are usually quite obvious.

By now, a majority of all work tasks should be identified; defined as to type of work; grouped within each function based on work type; and annual cost per task calculated. Inform the participants that you will be looking to form teams to plan the elimination of non-value tasks and each participant will be <u>invited</u> to participate on at least one team that will be set up within each work function to address their non-value tasks marked for elimination. Depending on the number of non-value tasks identified, the formation of multiple teams within a function may be required. This will provide an opportunity for everyone to participate on at least one team. If time permits, use the opportunity of this session to form the initial group of teams to select which non-value tasks they will address first, second, third, etc. If time does not permit, schedule another session—focused solely on the formation of the desired teams and the prioritization of which non-value tasks will be scheduled for elimination first, second, third and so on.

Step #2 – Identify Improvement Opportunities

"The obscure we see eventually. The completely obvious, it seems, takes longer." —Edward R. Murrow

Just the simple process of identifying non-value work tasks, will provide you with an abundance of improvement opportunities. You have just completed *Step 1 Task Analysis, Brainstorm with the Experts* and with their help and that of your leadership team you have identified several tasks for possible elimination. At this point you have gathered the labor costs associated with each of these tasks and in doing so have adequate data to begin the prioritization of tasks marked for elimination. Although you might be inclined to simply go after the most costly of the non-value tasks—a word of caution— as this should not be the only criteria used to prioritize the elimination process. Other factors to consider include resource requirements and potential risk to remaining processes. And, sometimes the priority might just be the improvement that generates little to no savings but is just the right thing to do.

Another thing to keep in mind while you're still in the early stages of getting business fit is the need to get some easy or quick wins under your belt to keep the momentum and excitement going throughout your organization in support of your fitting process. Early successes and celebrations can become the springboard to even greater wins. Look at it from this perspective…if you choose an improvement opportunity only because it has the potential to deliver great savings but the savings may not be realized for several months—you stand the risk of losing the momentum and excitement of your leadership team and workforce along the way. "hurry up and wait" will not sustain the excitement and momentum you're after here…not when most of us are programmed for more instant gratification. So, the ultimate approach would be to have a mix of smaller quick win projects to coincide with the larger more substantial wins. This will bode well in ensuring that the excitement and momentum will be reinforced with mini-celebrations—leading up to the "big win" that awaits months down the road.

In any case, you'll want to establish some guidelines as to how improvement opportunities will be identified, quantified, documented, prioritized, and how resources are allocated, improvements verified, results validated, and teams rewarded. For a simple procedure to build from, please refer to *Exhibit D Improvement Submittal Process*

Given the opportunity, your employees can play a key role in creating a more productive work environment while eliminating waste and enhancing customer focus and satisfaction. Once all non-value work has been identified and earmarked for elimination, empower your brainstorming participants to help reassign work tasks to achieve a fair distribution of work as individuals are transitioned away from the non-value work and over to more meaningful value-added work. They can also play a key role in cross-training and setting up task back-up owners where needed. Engage them!

Building Your Teams

"Never doubt that a small group of thoughtful and committed people can change the world. Indeed. It's the only thing that ever has." —Margaret Mead

Team Members

Teams are most successful when they have a vested interested in achieving their team goals and objectives. Team members should include individuals who actually perform the work tasks that have been identified for potential elimination. Most importantly, each team member must be willing to participate—no slackers— no forced participation. The size of the teams should be kept to a maximum of eight participants and minimum of five including the team leader. If unable to come up with at least five team members due to the size of your organization, work with the size you have—as long as there are at least three participants including the team leader. If the team is still too small…welcome to the team!

Team Leader

"When it's all over, it's not who you were. It's whether you made a difference." —Bob Dole

The team leader should be someone from within the work function where the task is being eliminated, that has earned the trust and respect of the team members. I have had great success with supervisors serving as team leaders because they usually work closely with the team members and have ownership of a portion or all of the function— yet are stilled viewed as "not yet management." This is also a great opportunity for your supervisors to further develop their team leadership skills. It is imperative that the team leader demonstrates good leadership and communication skills and the ability to instill fairness giving equal attention and support to each team member. Therefore, I highly recommend that your team leaders and their team members participate in some formalized introductory team training introducing them to the basic roles and responsibilities of a team. Check with your Human Resource representative, or there are inexpensive off the shelf courses as well as web-based online courses that will suffice.

Team Charter

A team charter must be developed. To what extent the team charter will encompass, depends on the scope of what the team is setting out to accomplish. Key identifiers of a thorough team charter include:

- A project description
- A problem statement
- An established business case
- An establish goal statement based on your

business case

- Potential constraints or limitations such as boundaries, time, etc.
- What is in and out of scope of the project
- The team members and required resources (team sponsor, champion, leader, facilitator, members, resource specialist, timekeeper, scribe, etc.) as deemed appropriate to the scope of the project
- Clearly defined and assigned team member roles
- The customers (internal and external)
- Project CTQs (critical to quality)
- A simple "high level" process map
- Benefits and expected deliverables (tangible & intangible)
- A proposed timeline for project completion

Choose which identifiers add the most value to your particular project. The more used the better, but don't force-use identifiers just for the sake of their existence. Sometimes less is more.

Team Focus

Your initial teams will not be tasked with seeking out and identify opportunities for improvement as the opportunities have already been identified through your prior brainstorming sessions and task analysis process. The primary focus of the team at this point should be to ensure that team members:

- Mutually understand the team's goal
- Are committed to the team's goal
- Clearly understand their roles
- Decisions are made based on facts not emotions
- Know and understand the ground rules of the team meetings
- Actively participate in dialog and team tasks

Additional Guidelines to Ensure the Success of the Team

"When dealing with people, remember you are not dealing with creatures of logic, but creatures of emotion." —Dale Carnegie

The team leader must ensure that all meetings are scheduled to accommodate active participation by <u>all</u> team members. Minutes should be taken at each meeting and distributed promptly following each meeting. The team leader must ensure that personalities do not interfere with team progress during scheduled meetings. Decisions shall be fact-based, no idea is a bad idea, quantity over quality and everybody should have the opportunity to be heard, but not dominate allocation of time at the meeting. The meetings must remain productive only being scheduled if there are matters that require group discussions and or decision making. When it is determined that a meeting is needed, stick to the date and time chosen, avoiding excessive rescheduling and or cancellations. All scheduled meetings shall begin and end on time.

Team assignments must be fairly distributed and closely monitored to ensure they are completed within a reasonable time frame. Team members that consistently miss scheduled meetings, arrive late, do not perform or actively participate, or add no value to the team shall be replaced without hesitation. The team leader is tasked with keeping management apprised of team accomplishments on a regular and timely basis. Finally, the team leader is responsible to ensure that team members are acknowledged, recognized and rewarded for achieving key milestones and eventual project success.

Step #3 – Establish a Quality Management System

"Great things are not done by impulse, but by a series of small things brought together." —Vincent Van Gogh

Facilitating a task analysis is an excellent starting point to engage your organization in getting business fit. Now that you have established momentum throughout your organization, let's look at the foundation you will need to build on to further develop your business' fitness.

Most organizations of any reasonable size already have a Quality Group with oversight of a sound quality management system. If by chance you don't I highly recommend that you give serious thought in establishing yours. Don't take the easy way out by sticking the oversight of Quality and Continuous Improvement with Engineering, Human Resources, or worse yet Operations. Your Quality Group should be independent of the functions they will be assessing, auditing and improving and be championed by a true Quality professional with a strong passion for Quality, Customer Focus and Continuous Improvement. This champion should be flexible, have a proven track record and possess exceptional communication skills. Having a background in Industrial Engineering or Business Management is a plus…as you'll want them to relate well with the sharp minds of Engineers as well as possess an entrepreneurial spirit.

In establishing your Quality Management System (QMS) you have several options. Many successful organizations have sought the guidelines of ISO 9001: 2000 (soon to become ISO 9001: 2008) while others have embraced Malcolm Baldrige criteria for Performance Excellence. I have had the advantage of working with both as well as some excellent "home grown" Fortune 500 versions. The key to success with any QMS is the level of commitment that you instill from the top down. If you embrace it so will your leadership team and your workforce. It's really that simple. You don't necessarily need to hire an expensive consulting firm to help you win the Malcolm Baldrige Quality Award in order to succeed with your QMS. You do however need the will of your people, their desire and your 100% support to not only succeed, but succeed long-term.

Creating Your In-House Quality Management System

To borrow from the ISO 9001: 2000 standards, I would recommend that your QMS be defined based on the following quality principles:

- Continual focus on your customer
- Continual leadership
- Involving your people
- Applying the process approach
- Applying the system approach to management
- Continual improvement

- Taking the factual approach to decision making

- Establishing mutually beneficial supplier relationships

These principles must be embraced by your leadership team from the top down and engrained within your culture—to fully succeed in getting business fit. You will need to bring together your leaders and top managers to regularly review your QMS to ensure that these principles continually apply and are adhered to throughout your organization. Unfortunately, if you were to reach out to those organizations that have already achieved QMS certification and ask them how they facilitate their reviews—in most cases you will find that:

- Their reviews are once annually

- They are combined with some other management meeting

- Someone from mid-management who owns the QMS facilitates the review

- Only management is present or actively participates

- The review takes (at best) about an hour

- The QMS owner gives an overview/update of the QMS

- Participants ask a few probing questions

- The QMS owner is politely thanked then excused

- The QMS owner creates (usually embellished) minutes that reflect the review

- The QMS owner and their peers do little leading up to the annual surveillance audits until the eleventh hour when they scramble to ready themselves

- The external auditor facilitates the audit and provides a list of minor nonconformities and observations

- The QMS owner comes up with a plan to address the minor nonconformities and observations

- The QMS owner submits the corrective action plan to their QMS registrar for approval

- The QMS registrar accepts the corrective action plan

- The QMS owner goes back to their "real" job and everything goes back to prior status quo for the next 11 months and the next annual Management Review

This is not to say that all organizations who have achieved QMS certification conduct themselves in this manner... many have embraced their QMS as part of their culture and have reaped great rewards as a result. But, those that do are too few and those that don't are too many. If you only pursue a QMS certification for marketing purposes or just to satisfy a customer requirement, know this: in most instances where this is the approach, the amount of time that you put into correcting errors, addressing customer complaints, and performing rework—on average—costs your bottom-line as much as 10 times more than the direct cost of a well managed QMS. In other words, you're better off morally and financially—to just do it right the first time. Embrace your QMS and do it right.

Management Review

"Only when we have something to value, will we have something to evaluate…and we cannot value something that we cannot share, exchange and examine." —Lee Shulman

At least quarterly, you and your leadership team should come together to review the success of your quality management system (QMS). The review should include assessing opportunities for organizational and process improvement. A set agenda should be developed and adhered to at each of the quality reviews. A typical agenda should include the following topics*:

Review Input

- Follow-up Actions Taken as a Result of Prior Audits or Business Group Reviews

- Outcomes Following Receipt of Customer Feedback (including complaints)

- Corrective Action and Preventive Action (CAPA)

- Business Changes that can Affect the QMS

- Recommendations for Improvement (i.e., tasks eliminated, etc.)

Review Output

- Improvement of the Effectiveness of the QMS and its Processes

- Improvement of Product or Services and Services Relative to Customer Requirements

- Resource Needs with an Emphasis on Staff Development

*Source: ISO 9001: 2000 Quality Manual Criteria

Non-leadership representatives (task experts) from each function should also be invited to actively participate in the review process.

Follow-up actions from prior audits/reviews—

If you're adhering to a sound QMS you are facilitating internal assessments of your systems and processes to ensure adherence and opportunities for improvement. This agenda item topic is intended to review the results of these internal assessments' follow up actions.

Outcomes Following Receipt of Customer Feedback (including complaints)—

How is customer feedback and complaints documented and followed up on? Who owns this process? The owner should be present at management review to answer these crucial questions and to share with top management, specifically—feedback received and complaints documented since the last management review and tie into the CAPA process.

In regards to customer feedback, if you're not taking advantage of both internal and external surveys, you need to start doing so. I can't imagine an organization of any size not taking advantage of customer feedback and acting on it with a sense of urgency. Surveys can be easily outsourced to third-party administrators who can facilitate them, taking the hassle out of doing so internally along with culling the results and establishing a sense of confidentiality for participants.

Corrective Action and Preventive Action (CAPA)—

CAPA is an area that I've found to be surprisingly neglected in many organizations. Plenty of time appears to be allocated to "react" to complaints and work errors, but little if any time is set aside for a "proactive" approach to root cause analysis and the prevention of reoccurrence. All incidents should be logged and criteria established for initiating both corrective AND preventive actions. If logged, repetitive incidents will become obvious. Obvious incidents will undergo an analysis to determine the root cause so that the problem can be corrected once and for all—thereby preventing reoccurrence. There are plenty of examples of Corrective Action Reports or "CARs" that you can access via the internet or you can email me at gary@fitcert.com and I'll be glad to send you the latest version I use. Having this on the Management Review agenda helps to emphasize your commitment to corrective and preventive actions and the need to take a timely and proactive approach to complaints, errors or quality incidents.

Business Changes that can affect the QMS—

This can be a wide range of things but some more obvious affects to consider might be reorganizing or restructuring. In today's worsening economy, many companies have been forced to make major adjustments to how they conduct business—faced with a reduction in workforce, a weakening customer base, increased costs to produce and deliver goods and services, etc. These affects can directly impact your QMS and its effectiveness. Management review is the forum to explore these challenges to seek both short- and long-term solutions.

Recommendations for Improvement (i.e., tasks eliminated, etc.)—

Management review is an ideal forum to invite team members to present their recommendations for continual improvement. It is also the appropriate time to prioritize the proposed improvements, allocate required resources and issue authorization to proceed. I would highly suggest that you also set aside time to acknowledge the progress or success of previously approved projects.

Improvement of the Effectiveness of the QMS and its Processes—

Is your QMS working? Is your existing quality policy and are your quality objectives still current—do they address your "current" needs? Are your quality objectives being met? Is process performance improving? Are timely actions taken to address quality problems? Are you adequately capturing and following up on customer feedback and complaints? Are your QMS internal audits and assessments being taken seriously and are they consistent? These are all questions that once answered, will help you determine if in fact your QMS is working and what adjustments and further actions might be needed to improve the effectiveness of your QMS and its processes.

Improvement of Product or Services and Services Relative to Customer Requirements—

When considering the improvement of product or service, have you established and documented quality objectives and requirements for all your products and services? Have you established processes, documents, and committed resources specific to the product or service? Have you established verification, validation, monitoring, inspections and test activities specific to your product or service and the criteria for acceptance? Do you retain adequate records needed to provide evidence that the realization processes and resulting product or service meet requirements? You'll want to answer "yes" to these questions as well but if you are unable to at this point, now's the right time (and forum) to get started on improving your processes—so that you have adequate data to begin improving your products or services. Let's not put the cart before the horse.

As for improving services relative to customer requirements, here's another place where you need to ensure that you have well defined processes first. Have you captured your customer's specific requirements including delivery and post-delivery activities? What about statutory and regulatory requirements related to the product or service? Have you documented other product or service information such as contracts, order handling, amendments, customer feedback, etc.? Again, get your processes in order before you seek to improve them and or the products or services you provide.

Resource Needs with an Emphasis on Staff Development—

Are your leaders and your workforce able to do what's required of them? In other words, are they competent? How do you know that they are? Have they been properly educated and trained? Do they have the level of skills and experience required to do their assigned work tasks effectively? Do you have a formal process of documenting or measuring the effectiveness of their work? Are they aware of the relevance and importance of their work activities and how they contribute to the achievement of quality objectives? Do you maintain appropriate records of education, training, skills and experience? Having answers to all of these questions is a start, but are the answers yes or no? If any of your answers are "no" you'll want to initiate some brainstorming at this point in the agenda to identify solutions with reasonable timelines to change the "no" to a resounding "yes" sooner rather than later.

Management Review can be as simple or as complicated as you choose to make it. Simplicity always wins out and assures you that your leaders and workforce will understand and better embrace your QMS. I have discovered that many organizations initially choose to establish their own in-house criteria for a QMS but the more successful ones eventually seek to embrace the guidelines of ISO, Malcolm Baldrige or some other formalized criteria. This is something you may want to consider once you believe you have exhausted all efforts in getting business fit and wish to raise the quality bar. If you're interested, I know some great firms that provide ISO implementation services or you can consider the Fit Certification process. To learn more about QMS certification options, please visit my website at *http:// fitcert.com/.*

"You can take great people, highly trained and motivated, and put them in a lousy system and the system will win every time."—Geary Rummler, CEO Performance Design Lab

Document Your Processes and Standardize

In line with your quality management system, you'll want to establish a standardized format for your controlled documents such as standard operating procedures, work instructions, forms, etc. To determine which SOPs and WIs to commit to first, begin with those work tasks that you've previously identified as *Value Work*. No sense wasting your time creating controlled documentation for work tasks that you've already targeted for elimination.

As far as referencing your documented processes as either a standard operating procedure (SOP) or work instruction (WI) I've always preferred the term work instruction. It sounds less formal and is exactly what it is—instructions on how to perform the work. As opposed to the more formal term of standard operating procedure which sounds sterile, formal and somewhat intimidating.

For the sake of my preference going forward I will use the term work instructions and I recommend that you do the same. Most likely, your work force will be more open to the term work instruction as well.

Keep in mind when developing your WIs, they need to be precise, current and easy to read and follow. Avoid the technical jargon. Your best bet will be to have those that are or will be performing the work tasks, write the WIs, or at least have them participate in the process.

Each WI must then be assigned to an "owner" that will capture necessary updates to ensure the document remains current. All WIs should also be regularly evaluated by a qualified quality auditor to ensure that employees adhere to them, and that they remain current and easily accessible. As a new WI is developed or existing ones updated, all individuals or groups that might be impacted (directly or indirectly) must be made aware and or trained as to the new process they govern.

If you haven't already, you may want to look into outsourcing the administration of your standard operating procedures and WIs to a third party administrator. There are several great third-party administrators that can provide this service freeing up your resources to focus on more value-added tasks. My company [business fit associates] provides this service in a web-based format for easy access, update and control. If you are interested we'd love to provide you with additional information. Just drop us a line at: sales@fitcert.com.

Step #4 – Educate and Train

"Nobody's a natural. You work hard to get good and then work hard to get better." —Paul Coffey

As the only constant is change you must prepare your organization to welcome change and quickly and seamlessly adapt to it. To do so you're going to need a sound awareness, education and training process. Furthermore, the workforce of today expects more opportunities to demonstrate their talents and abilities. They strive for opportunities to learn and contribute at a higher level than just what their typical job duties call for. This drive must be embraced and nurtured to ensure that individual capabilities are maximized for their benefit and that of your organization. Just having controlled documents such as WIs and SOPs is not enough. They will serve no value if they spend their days tucked away in a fancy binder on a shelf. They need to be easily accessible, easy to read and reviewed for updates regularly. They should be incorporated into your training curriculum and serve as the primary source for introducing individuals to their assigned tasks and the role they and their tasks play in overall work processes.

Using your new WIs and training curriculum, you'll want to develop a training plan. The development of training plans should be a collaborative effort between Human Resources, your task experts and leadership team.

The Training Plan

There are two primary levels of a training that I define as Corporate and Specific. Corporate training encompasses your entire organization while Specific training targets your individual organizational units (groups, departments, etc.). The elements of your training plan should include:

- An approved budget and allocated resources—to ensure success.
- Background information—purpose for the training plan.
- Training status—training completed to date.
- Training mission—what you hope to achieve.
- Training approach and methodology—type of training, delivery, participants.
- Course descriptions—current and proposed.
- Training schedules—dates, times and locations.
- Learning goals and objectives—linked to organizational goals and objectives.
- Testing process—to measure success.
- Evaluation Process—to continually improve on curriculum.
- Reports—to inform the organization on training outcomes, future plans, etc.

The development and execution of a sound training plan should be a top priority in your organization. Having one is no longer considered a nicety—it is now a means of survival where employers are faced with exorbitant costs associated with their continual struggle to find and retain good talent.

Training, Educating & Learning

According to the Research Institute of America and several other sources, knowledge retention from classroom training degrades to 59%, 30 minutes after course completion, to 33% after 48 hours, and to less than 10% after a few weeks. Considering these facts, it is imperative that you incorporate a "mix" into your training plan. What I mean by a mix is to follow up your "classroom" instruction with a combination of sound coaching, practice, application of learning, feedback and reinforcement. The focus is educating and learning as opposed to simply going through the motions of training your workforce and leaders to meet the requirements of a training plan. Research also shows a 45% to 110% improvement in performance when utilizing a "mixed" approach when training and educating for measured results.

Back-Up Task Owners

With the exception of a few, most organizations where I have facilitated a task analysis had previously failed to recognize the value of identifying and retaining back-up owners. They also failed to realize the risk associated with this failure. The reasons provided for the lack of focus in identifying, assigning and preparing back-ups always sounded familiar:

- We'll cross that bridge when we get to it…

- That's what supervisors are for…to jump in when they're need…

- If someone is out, that's what overtime is for…

- If we get in a bind…we just use more temps…

- Etc., etc.

Do any of these excuses sound familiar to you?

Poor planning when it comes to resources can be more costly than just the extra cost of overtime or bringing in a few temps. If you rely on the four options above you are creating more than just additional costs… you are creating unnecessary risk. Think about it…do you really believe that pulling a supervisor away from their critical or necessary work is a wise option. What possible neglect might occur by making that supervisor unavailable to your operation while they fill in for a lower level void…at a higher pay rate I might add? What about the overtime option…paying folks at time and a half… not only does it add unnecessary costs to your bottom-line and reduce profits…individuals on overtime increase the risk of errors, damaging product and equipment, unsafe practices that can lead to costly injuries, reduced productivity, etc. And, finally…what about relying on temps to fill unplanned voids…good option? Well let's see…usually you're not just paying an hourly rate…you're paying a "mark-up" to the temp agency…and allot more. And, in many instances you're bringing in less skilled workers that may not be as familiar with your business, your product or service, your processes, your equipment, or your customers. Do you think this option might lead to more risk with errors, damage, safety, productivity, etc.? Absolutely! Your best, or in my opinion ONLY option is in establishing qualified back-up owners for key tasks...period. Having said that I must clarify one point when it comes to using temps. I am in no way slamming temps or temp agencies—they do serve a tremendous need in many organizations...probably in yours and they have in mine. Just be sure to use them as a result of a real cost-effective or planned need, as opposed to the result of poor planning. In fact they are an excellent source of securing talent in advance of future vacancies.

"Competitive advantage for an organization is in its ability to enhance what it uniquely does best and apply it to the next business opportunity." —The ASTD Training and Development Handbook, Fourth Edition

Step #5 – Reward Success

"Without inspiration the best powers of the mind remain dormant, there is a fuel in us which needs to be ignited with sparks." —Johann Gottfried Von Herder

I have always been a firm believer that you get better results out of your workforce if you reward good behavior as opposed to expecting good behavior and punishing bad behavior. A carefully orchestrated incentive program can have a substantially positive impact on your bottom line while igniting that spark that empowers your workforce to willingly engage in continuous improvement efforts. Unfortunately, many executives still hold on to the argument "why should we reward folks for doing what we already pay them to do?" And, "if they don't do what we pay them to do how and when we want them to, then we simply get rid of them and hire someone else that will".

The workforce of today is just not wired the same as management of today. The workforce of today is extremely talented but they are also much more technical. If not continually challenged they tend to lose interest quicker than we do and they just rarely stand for disciplinary threats of any kind. They will quite on you at the drop of a hat because they know they have skills that are in demand just down the street and can start working there almost immediately. The old ways of remaining loyal to one company throughout your career ended with the

Bob Hope generation. You might find some of us Baby Boomers still hanging on to this old tradition, but there are fewer and fewer who do. The workforce of today gets antsy and wants to be challenged not pushed and they want to move around and try new things. If they can't find new things within your company to keep them challenged, they will go elsewhere…period.

If you are a culprit of holding on to the "old way of thinking" you're out of touch with reality and you're part of the problem. You need to start asking "why not" rather than "why" when it comes to rewarding ideas that affect cost savings, quality, productivity, process improvement, revenue-generation, improved employee motivation and positive morale. Rewards don't always have to be monetary although they are usually more desirable. Rewards can come in the form of merchandise with your company's logo, gift certificates, lunch with management, a quarterly award luncheon and points toward purchasing more expensive items from catalogs. There are companies out there like *Grapevine Designs* in Kansas City, Kansas that specialize in setting up a simple but innovative web-based reward program that can accommodate all of the above.

I believe as human beings we naturally seek out meaningful work. And I believe we all desire to do a good job. I believe it's extremely rare to discover an employee who comes to work with the sole purpose of performing poorly. And, I believe everyone has the need to feel wanted and appreciated. Sure, all your employees are being compensated for the work they are tasked with and you probably already have some type of incentive program that rewards employees when certain goals are met or exceeded. That's great—don't end those programs. Instead, I'm suggesting that you add an additional incentive program. One that rewards individuals and teams who go above and beyond—as opposed to rewarding everyone for the success of a few such as with Gain Sharing where everyone's rewarded whether they rightfully contributed or not in meeting or exceeding certain productivity goals or objectives. Again, Gain Sharing is a great program where you have all winners or all losers and satisfies the psychotherapists. When it comes to business however, I just don't buy in to the concept they push that "we must reward everyone or no one" or "we can't have winners and losers…everyone must be treated as winners…" approach in life. Instead, I ask, what about those super achievers…those that really do go the extra mile? How will you continue to inspire them to deliver when they eventually realize they don't have to—that they can just fall in line behind all the other poor to average performers and still be rewarded when meeting that productivity (Gain Share) goal? I say give them something to strive for as individuals like being recognized for their exceptional performance—and they will not let you down. They will not only flourish, they will multiply and surpass any expectations that you might have today. Incent them and as you do, others that are less motivated will be inspired. The return on the investment can and will be substantial.

Example Incentive Program

"A pat on the back is only a few vertebrae removed from a kick in the pants, but is miles ahead in results." —V. Wilcox

I'd like to share with you a past success I experienced firsthand with an incentive program that rewarded individuals and teams for achieving success with continuous improvement initiatives that will knock your socks off. The incentive program was rolled out in an organization that I worked with that rewarded individuals and teams who identified opportunities for improvement that resulted in substantial savings. This program was so successful that within the first six months following its roll out, $1.7 million in savings was validated by the finance group as bottom line savings. One team alone comprised of five members succeeded in identifying an improvement opportunity that resulted in $1.1 million in savings and split an incentive check for $10,000. Two other teams were successful in saving hundreds of thousands of dollars and split incentive checks for $5,000 and $2,500 while two individuals received incentive checks—one for $5,000 and the other for $2,500.

When word got out about the amount of monies awarded, application submittals for improvement opportunities quadrupled in the first 45-days following the award ceremony and continued at a steady pace thereafter. In just under 12 months more than $5.7 million in projected savings was identified. So, let's do some quick calculations. At the end of the first year, $35,000 was awarded to individuals and teams who succeeded in identifying opportunities for improvement that resulted in $5.7 million in projected savings. That's a substantial ROI when you do the math. Do you still think rewarding individuals and teams independent of programs like Gain Share is not a good idea? Where else in ANY investment market can you expect returns of this magnitude, especially in today's challenging economy?

Another naysayer argument is "well, these projected savings are soft not hard bottom line savings…I don't see this improvement reducing headcount…" That's usually not the case but even if this statement were true and allot of times—especially when an organization and its workforce are first introduced to efforts to identify improvement opportunities—it can be, would you choose to forego the soft savings simply because they're not clearly hard savings—in a business economy of today, where the slightest advantage over your competitor can literally save you from bankruptcy? A vast majority of the improvement discoveries come from "hidden" waste that can remain undetected by leadership if not exposed by your task experts. You have only to gain by recognizing and rewarding any type of improvements in your organization—hard or soft.

A few more things to say about soft versus hard savings that I just got to put out there. What do you think the response would be from your workforce if you told them that you are only interested in rewarding ideas that reduce headcount? Do you anticipate them clambering to get their ideas on paper and submitted for consideration if the only objective is to reduce headcount—which possibly could mean placing their own job security in jeopardy? Let's be real here…the goal must be to eliminate non-value tasks so that individuals can focus their time and effort on tasks that add value from the customer's perspective. If you insist on remaining narrow minded and only consider hard savings—you're never going to achieve a lean and fit business. You'll get short-term quick fix wins at the expense of ignoring long-term sustainable improvement. You'll continue to churn top talent out of your organization and in to those who value their contributions to the bottom line—hard or soft. So, get over yourself and yesterday's thinking or update your resume—as you may need it sooner than you think. Too many organizations out there have already figured out what it takes to get business fit and many of them are your competition standing right behind you—breathing down your neck. I know this…I sold them copies of *Getting Business Fit* too.

Conclusion

"Quality is never an accident; it is always the result of high intention, sincere effort, intelligent direction and skillful execution; it represents the wise choice of many alternatives."
—William A. Foster

By now it should be a no brainer for you to realize the fruits of your labor. The brainstorming exercises should have uncovered many opportunities for process improvement and the elimination of waste and non-value work. By eventually eliminating the non-value work, you will increase the availability of valued resources to transition over to value work. The increase in value work resources will result in increased productivity. The increased productivity will mean an increased revenue stream. The increased revenue stream can lead to business growth, stabilized profit planning, availability to better reward and recognize your workforce, and should keep your shareholders smiling.

By following my simple five steps to getting business fit, you will experience measured improvements in quality, productivity and customer satisfaction and a decrease in errors, damages and defects. Moral will go up, absenteeism and tardiness down. The potential to continually improve processes and eliminate waste will continue to be unlimited—now that you have educated yourself and your workforce on how to identify, quantify and eliminate waste in your organization.

At this point I highly suggest that you go back to step one and re-read through all five steps. When you're finished, secure additional copies of this book and present them to your leadership team to read. After you have provided ample time for them to receive and review their copy of this book, schedule a meeting to plan your first task analysis brainstorming session and let's start getting business fit.

If you have any follow up questions regarding this book or any aspect of it, please do not hesitate to email me at gary@fitcert.com. In the interim, you can find additional helpful tips to getting your fit program going in your organization in the Appendix that follows.

I wish you and your organization all the success and look forward to hearing about your successes that I may share in my next book "*Staying Business Fit*."

"Motivation is our beginning, commitment our journey and character our fuel...when success is our destiny."
—Gary King

APPENDIX

Exhibit A:
TASK ANALYSIS SPREADSHEET

FUNCTION	TASK	TASK OWNER	BACKUP OWNER	HOURLY RATE	WORK TYPE	CUSTOMER	TASK FREQ	HOURS	FORMAL TRAIN.	WI/SOPs	ANNUAL COST
Docks	Unload	Jim / Diane	Bob	$26	R	Ops	Daily	2	N	N	$27,040
Purchasing	Order Supplies	Mary	N/A	$14	R	Admin	Week	4	N	N	$2,912

With this example spreadsheet you can gather a few immediate learnings:

1. The first task listed is performed by more than one task owner and a back-up task owner has been designated. This is a good start as many organizations overlook the need to have designated back-up owners to help with peak times and in the absence or unavailability of the task owner (on vacation, out sick, helping out in another department, in training, etc.). As you can see with the second task listed, no back-up task owner has been designated. This should become a priority at some point to ensure that someone is designated and receives adequate training and periodic (direct) exposure to the task so that they can remain at the ready should they need to step in to perform this task.

2. Another learning is the "type" of work that has been noted for both tasks which is "R" for required. In other words, this work is essential to keep the

business flowing. It may not add any direct benefit to the customer but it serves a purpose in the function. When looking for improvements to "Required" tasks, seek opportunities to reduce time/frequency, process steps, documentation, and resources without jeopardizing the quality of work output.

3. Note that under the header "Formal Training" the response is "N" for No. This means that the individual performing the task has not received any formal training—on the job or otherwise. Or, whatever training they may have received may not be sufficient. Training is crucial to ensure that people work at peak performance, have the appropriate skills and tools to accomplish their work tasks, clearly understand their roles and responsibilities and the desired deliverables. If it's not formalized and documented, it doesn't exist.

4. Under the header WI-SOP or Work Instructions or Standard Operating Procedures the response is "N" for No. This means that no formal process has been documented to serve as a guide for those performing these work tasks. Without written documentation to support work tasks, you have limited opportunity to adequately train your workforce to perform to standards and expectations; you risk inconsistencies in processes, possible omission of key steps, errors in work output, inability to properly evaluate work performance, etc. All required and value work should have a current work instruction that is regularly reviewed and updated accordingly. Also, every work

instruction—like each task, should have a designated owner.

5. Finally, under the last heading—annual cost you can quickly see which task has a greater cost to the function and organization as a whole. This may help you prioritize which tasks you may want to address first as a priority over others to gain the most improvements or capture the greatest savings. However, there may be instances with other driving factors whereas you may seek to reduce or eliminate a task with a lower savings than another. An example of factors might include: priorities established by executive management or an external customer; intentions or the need to secure "quick wins"; to meet certain regulatory requirements; etc. In any case, reduction and possible elimination of "non-value" work should be your ultimate objective, followed by "non-work" and improvement to "required work."

APPENDIX

Exhibit B:
CHECKLIST FOR BRAINSTORMING SESSION

Pre-Brainstorming

1. Define your problem and purpose for the session (what are you setting out to accomplish?).

2. Determine the structure and venue you will be following.

3. Select a facilitator (remember if you're going with your own in-house facilitator and it's not you, choose someone that already has demonstrated their skills and abilities as a facilitator, or ensure that they successfully complete formalized facilitation training course work).

4. Identify your participants targeting a group size of about a dozen.

5. Identify all required equipment (laptop, projector, flip chart stand, etc.).

6. Identify and secure supplies (flip charts, broad felt tipped markers, post-it-note pads, etc.).

7. Choose the right location (conference room), layout options, etc.

8. Design an informal atmosphere to create a comfortable environment.

9. Choose the right timing for the session (not during peak, etc.).

10. Choose the best time of day (I like 08:30 on Wednesday mornings).

Brainstorming

1. The facilitator arrives early, at least 30-minutes prior to the schedule start time for the session.

2. The session begins on time—whether or not all participants are present.

3. The facilitator welcomes the participants as they arrive and engages in casual conversation.

4. The facilitator introduces their self as a kick-off to self-introductions.

5. The facilitator goes over some safety and housekeeping items such as the location of exits and restrooms.

6. The facilitator explains the purpose for the session and the session objectives.

7. The facilitator reviews and explains the brainstorming

rules: no idea is a bad idea, suspend judgment, no criticism, etc.

8. The group brainstorms the problem (the objective is to go for quantity not quality—we can evaluate later, offer of solutions freely, record the ideas, display ideas using post-it-note flip charts in full view, assign numbers to each flip chart page and listed idea, include one minute breaks to aid cross-fertilization, etc.).

9. Closure (when preparing to end the session, make it obvious. Provide at least a five or ten minute warning).

10. Distribute minutes and the updated list of ideas within 24 hours from each session.

Post-Brainstorming:

1. Review all ideas to select those that easily stand out as doable actions.

2. Using a ranking system can be most helpful—such as a "3" for great ideas, "2" for okay to good ideas and "1" for those ideas that appear less doable due to cost or time constraints, or commitment of too many resources.

3. Use reverse brainstorming to capture any potential for idea failure.

4. Determine costs; acceptability to management, staff and customers; the legality and practicality;

time and resource commitments; sense of urgency (if commitment is delayed will the opportunity be jeopardized?

5. Select best ideas.

Does and Don'ts of Brainstorming

Does—

- Be sensitive to participant's initial fears and or shyness to participate early in the process. Don't force participation—let it happen gradually and naturally.

- Encourage mobility—some folks (like me) think better on their feet—walking around or pacing.

- Ensure that participants have made proper arrangements for coverage within their work function to avoid any negative impact caused by the participant's absence from operations.

- Encourage an informal atmosphere free of criticism, fear, blame, insults, interruptions, or inhibition.

Don'ts—

- Do not allow the sessions to go on too long…keep the sessions within the scheduled timeframe.

- Interruptions should be nonexistent. Cell phones should be checked at the door or turned off. Sufficient breaks can be scheduled to allow participants to check in with their work functions periodically.

- Never attempt to use a tape recorder.
- Allow any form of criticism, fear, blame, insults, or interruptions.
- Allow the session to become a place to vent or complain about anything.

APPENDIX

Exhibit C:
KEY ELEMENTS OF A QUALITY
MANAGEMENT SYSTEM

4. Quality Management System

4.1 General Requirements
4.2 Documentation Requirements
    4.2.3 Control of Documents
    4.2.4 Control of Records

5. Management Responsibility

5.1 Management Commitment
5.2 Customer Focus
5.3 Quality Policy
5.4 Planning
5.5 Responsibility, Authority and Communication
5.6 Management Review

6. Resource Management

6.1 Provision of Resources
6.2 Human Resources
6.3 Infrastructure
6.4 Work Environment

7. Product Realization

7.1 Planning of Product Realization
7.2 Customer-Related Processes
7.3 Design and Development
7.4 Purchasing
7.5 Production and Service Provision
    7.5.1 Control of Production and Service Provision
    7.5.2 Validation of Processes for Production and Service Provision
    7.5.3 Identification and Traceability
    7.5.4 Customer Property
    7.5.5 Preservation of Product
7.6 Control of Monitoring and Measuring Devices

8. Measurement, Analysis and Improvement

8.1 General
8.2 Monitoring and Measurement
    8.2.1 Customer Satisfaction
    8.2.2 Internal Audit
    8.2.3 Monitoring and Measurement of Processes
    8.2.4 Monitoring and Measurement of Product
8.3 Control of Nonconforming Product
8.4 Analysis of Data
8.5 Improvement
    8.5.1 Continual Improvement
    8.5.2 Corrective Action
    8.5.3 Preventive Action

Source: The American Society for Quality, ASQ Quality Press

To what extent you choose to go in creating your Quality Management System is completely up to you. What I've provided above are the key elements that I've used in defining past quality management systems—which in their entirety meet the requirements of ISO 9001: 2000. You may wish to explore your options between the elements of ISO and criteria for Performance Excellence defined by the Malcolm Baldrige Quality Award program. They are both great resources in exploring your Quality Management System options.

If you've enjoyed the simplicity of the fit process in getting business fit than you may want to consider the *Fit Certification Process.* It's a Self-Implementation Certification process that is extremely simple to accomplish in a reasonable timeframe and can be tailored to your business and desired culture. *Fit Certification* offers companies of all sizes an alternative approach to achieving a higher level of quality and continual improvement standards without the high costs associated with other certification programs. And, should you still choose to pursue a certification program such as ISO 9001: 2000, the transition from *Fit Certification* to ISO can be accomplished seamlessly and at a greatly reduced cost—as *Fit Certification* meets the standards of ISO. For more information regarding our *Fit Certification* process, email business fit associates at: sales@fitcert.com and we'll arrange for you to speak to one of our Implementation Specialists.

APPENDIX

Exhibit D
IMPROVEMENT SUBMITTAL PROCESS

There are several ways to solicit improvement ideas from your workforce and leadership team. Whichever way you choose, you're going to want to formalize the process so that it's easy to meander through it successfully. Following are some tried and proven steps to help simplify and streamline an improvement submittal process.

- Team has identified an improvement opportunity.

- Team secures a submittal form created for this purpose.

- Team reviews the Work Instruction that governs the submittal process.

- Team completes the submittal form.

- Team reviews submittal form with immediate supervisor or designate.

- Supervisor or designate reviews submittal for completeness.

- Supervisor forwards completed submittal to designated Manager.

- Manager verifies the initial merit of the proposed improvement.

- If merited, Manager tentatively approves submittal.

- If no merit, Manager returns submittal to Team for additional info if warranted.

- If tentatively approved by Manager, and anticipated savings are less than $50,000, the Manager may authorize the Team to proceed with their improvement. If the anticipated savings is greater than $50,000 the submittal is forwarded to Executive Management for final approval to proceed.

- Based on pre-established criteria, Executive Management reviews and approves the submittal and the Team is issued an "approval to proceed" with their improvement.

- Team proceeds with the improvement.

Additional factors that must be considered with an improvement submittal process include:

1. Resource allocation—how will you ensure that adequate resources are committed to the improvement project?

2. Project management—what approach will you use to ensure the success of the project?

3. Improvement validation—how will you validate the success of the improvement?

4. Best practice—how will you share the learning from the success of the improvement?

5. Celebration—how will you recognize and reward the success of the improvement team?

Resource Allocation

To avoid the unnecessary competition for qualified resources I would suggest that you form a Resource Planning Council comprised of your executive leadership team. This team would meet to review and prioritize proposed improvement projects to gain a consensus on which projects have priority over others. Once priorities are established, a review of available resources is considered for allocation to the top priority projects. Without a unanimous consensus of the Resource Planning Council (with a tie broken by you), these priorities will not be changed or resources diverted.

Project Management

Ensuring that you have a formalized project management process will be essential to the success of the improvement itself. I have seen many projects managed by unskilled individuals with good intentions that delivered far less in improvement saving than the projects true potential. If you haven't already, give strong consideration to introducing Six Sigma Lean into your organization. The process of developing highly skilled in-house Six Sigma Green and Black Belts is a simple process—well worth the investment. Any project with projected savings greater than $50,000 should be led or mentored by (at least) a Six Sigma Green Belt. Projects exceeding $100,000 should have a Six Sigma Black Belt leading it. There are a lot of reputable organizations that provide good to excellent courses in Six Sigma Lean and

Belt certification. Go online and Google Six Sigma and you'll find the list to be nearly endless. The American Society for Quality (ASQ) is a great place to start too. Courses are available online, offsite or onsite at one of your business locations. I prefer the onsite option myself.

Improvement Validation

It's one thing to propose improvement savings and another to validate that they actually exist. Improvement submittals will be considered and approved based on the merit of the project and anticipated improvements or savings. Success will be based on the validation that measurable improvements or savings have been documented over a given timeframe. It is imperative that you involve a representative from your financial group to oversee the savings validation process. The process is already well defined within the Six Sigma DMAIC process that governs improvement projects but usually lacks the specific role of the Financial Representative in validating any savings.

Best Practice

During my days as an ISO auditor, there were countless times that I came across substantial improvements that remained confined within the walls of the given work unit when the improvements could have easily benefited other aspects of the organization. It shouldn't take an outsider to bring to your attention that you have best practices that aren't being shared throughout your organization. I have seen some really innovative processes that have resulted in substantial savings or that have delighted both internal and external customers—once they were made aware of them.

Consider establishing a Best Practice Team tasked with reviewing all new improvements and or improvements to existing processes, to gage possible benefits to other work units within your organization. And, have this team champion the collaboration amongst the leadership of your organizational functions—so that key learnings and best practices can be shared.

Celebration

As I have previously stated, I am a firm believer that you get better—longer-term results out of your workforce by rewarding good behavior as opposed to expecting good behavior and punishing bad behavior. Rewarding good behavior should include regular celebrations when key goals, objectives or major milestones are achieved. The celebration does not have to be anything grand… sometimes a simple acknowledgement amongst one's peers will suffice. I like to take advantage of key leadership meetings by having an agenda item set aside for the purpose of inviting those being recognized into the meetings to receive their recognition. I have worked with some organizations that have done more to formalize the celebration process by holding Quarterly Meetings where they recognize the accomplishments of others over a nice dinner. Some have chosen a well organized annual celebration or awards dinner where recipients are honored amongst key executives and fellow honorees.

However you choose to celebrate individual, team or organizational accomplishments just make sure that it doesn't become another one of those programs that are here today...gone tomorrow. If you're going to formalize how you celebrate major accomplishments in your organization, think it through, and commit to it whole heartedly and financially. Once you do, stay with it—no matter how financially challenging your organization may become in these troubling economic times. The reality is...you need your people thinking continuous improvement, best practices and waste elimination, now more than ever. If they know you're serious about it—as demonstrated by your commitment to the incentive and celebration process, they will come through for you in a big way.

"The formula for success is comprised of one part effort and one part relationship. Investing in one and not the other will only get you about half way, which would be...to "suc."
—Gary King